THE MARTIN LUTHER
PARENT AND CHILD CENTER
560 N. BROADWAY
BALTIMORE, MARYLAND 21205

Cultural Awareness
A Resource Bibliography

Cultural Awareness

A Resource Bibliography

By
Velma E. Schmidt
North Texas State University, Denton
and
Earldene McNeill
The Learning Tree, Dallas
Eastfield College, Mesquite

The National Association for the
Education of Young Children
Washington, D.C.

Photographs

Page   6 — Lynne Bruna, Steve Herzog, Florence Sharp
Page 18 — Jean Berlfein, Kevin McNeill, Sally Gale
Page 36 — Robert K. Smith, Arlie Jean Payne,
             Office of Economic Opportunity
Page 64 — Rick Reinhard, Candice Logue (2)
Page 88 — Ellen Levine Ebert, Dorothy Kay, Ellen Galinsky

Copyright © 1978. Second printing, 1979.
Velma E. Schmidt
and
Earldene McNeill

Library of Congress Catalog Card Number: 78-56983
ISBN Catalog Number: 0-912674-60-1
NAEYC #313
Printed in the United States of America.

Contents

	Page
Introduction	1
Ten Quick Ways to Analyze Children's Books for Racism and Sexism	3
Asian Americans	7
Books for Children	8
Resources for Adults	13
Books and Articles	13
Bibliographies	14
Catalogs	14
Periodicals	15
Materials and Experiences	16
Posters/Pictures	16
Records	16
Films/Filmstrips	17
Slides	17
Museums	17
Festivals/Fairs/Celebrations	17
Black Americans	19
Books for Children	20
Resources for Adults	28
Books and Articles	28
Bibliographies	31
Catalogs	31
Periodicals	31

	Page
Materials and Experiences	32
Posters/Pictures	32
Records	32
Films/Filmstrips	34
Slides	34
Dolls	34
Museums	34
Native Americans	37
Books for Children	38
Resources for Adults	49
Books and Articles	49
Bibliographies	54
Catalogs	54
Periodicals	55
Materials and Experiences	57
Posters/Pictures	57
Records	58
Films/Filmstrips	58
Slides	59
Dolls	59
Arts and Crafts	60
Museums	60
Ceremonials/Events	62
Spanish-Speaking Americans	65
Books for Children	66
Resources for Adults	72
Books and Articles	72
Bibliographies	77
Catalogs	79
Periodicals	80

	Page
Materials and Experiences	82
Posters/Pictures	82
Records	82
Films/Filmstrips	84
Slides	85
Dolls/Games/Flags/Kits	85
Museums	86
Festivals/Fairs/Celebrations	86
Multicultural Resources	89
Books for Children	90
Resources for Adults	93
Books and Articles	93
Bibliographies	96
Catalogs	98
Periodicals	101
Materials and Experiences	102
Posters	102
Records	102
Films/Filmstrips	103
Slides	105
Dolls	105
Museums	105
Resource Directory	107

Introduction

This multicultural bibliography grew out of a belief that relationships among people who are members of the various cultural groups in the United States can be improved. If you and I gain a knowledge of the history, beliefs, values, customs, and lifestyles of other cultures, then we can begin to understand individuals. Understanding can lead to acceptance—acceptance of diversity in living. Also, an appreciation of the contributions of a culture flows from understanding it. With a greater knowledge, understanding, and acceptance of diversity, interactions with each other can be sufficiently positive so that we can begin to actively support enhancement of human relations.

When do we begin to learn how to relate to persons from other cultures? Children develop their attitudes beginning the day of their birth. Parents have a responsibility to set an example in socialization with and in attitudes toward all adults and children. Adults in day care centers, nursery schools, and in the public schools have a responsibility to model positive attitudes toward all children and parents, and to expose children to the contributions of many cultures to American society. The responsibility of adults who work with children from other cultural backgrounds is to accept the beliefs and values of the children, and to build the program on these unique strengths, rather than requiring all children to conform to the values, behaviors, and beliefs of the dominant U.S. society. If children have the opportunity to grow in such an accepting group or school setting, both children and society will be enriched.

The feeling of pride in their lifestyles and own way of thinking is a powerful influence in helping children view themselves as worthy and valued human beings. Individuals who have a good feeling about themselves generally respond in loving and positive ways.

In addition to accepting all children, adults in early childhood development centers must have materials that enhance learning about various cultures. Since 1970, such materials for young children have been increasingly available. The quality and appropriateness of the materials range from excellent to poor.

The books and materials listed in this bibliography reflect the increase in these resources. The majority of them have been used by children and adults. The books for children have been used for several years with young children in The Learning Tree in Dallas. Teachers and college students from different cultures have used the adult books and materials in this bibliography and responded with their evaluations. Some of the books with older copyright dates are regarded as classics by many educators.

Conveying accurate information is the responsibility of any educator or publisher. However, not all educators and publishers take this responsibility seriously. Therefore, teachers/directors must know a culture in their communities well or ask someone from that culture to help evaluate and select materials.

Ideas expressed in reviews and annotations of materials and resources may not always agree with your experiences and beliefs. A list of criteria developed by the Council on Interracial Books for Children follows this introduction to aid you in evaluating resources listed in this bibliography as well as new materials published in the future. We encourage you to examine the vast amount of materials available, critically review them, and develop your own criteria for judging their use with the young children in your community. You can order catalogs from publishers and have your name placed on their mailing lists to receive notices of new multicultural materials. A Resource Directory is included at the end of this book so that you

Introduction

may contact sources directly, since prices are subject to change and materials sometimes are no longer available.

You can use this bibliography to select books and other materials for your library in your child development center, for your public school library, and for the public library in your community. How can children further develop an awareness of other cultures if multicultural materials are not available?

While materials can help develop cultural awareness, especially for young children, real experiences in interacting with children and adults of other cultural groups—engaging together in ethnic dances and songs; having an adult from that culture explain artifacts, dance, sing, or recite poetry; eating foods representative of a particular culture—are more meaningful. In fact, real experiences often stimulate children to read books to find out more about a new interest. Adults can use the resources listed in this book to plan for real experiences and increase their own cultural awareness. Suggested age levels for many of the books and materials are designated with overlapping age ranges as follows:

N—**Nursery, up to age 5**
K—**Kindergarten, ages 4 to 6**
P—**Primary, ages 5 to 9**
A—**Adult**

Young children cannot understand the complexity of feelings among persons of different cultures, but they can become aware of the many similarities and relatively few differences among individuals. Young children can begin to accept diversity in values, languages, and lifestyles in America, and can begin to appreciate the enriching quality of diversity in our society. Young children can learn to accept others and develop skills in relating to children and adults with different heritages.

Velma E. Schmidt
Earldene McNeill
June 1978

Ten Quick Ways to Analyze Children's Books for Racism and Sexism

Both in school and out, young children are exposed to racist and sexist attitudes. These attitudes—expressed over and over in books and in other media—gradually distort their perceptions until stereotypes and myths about minorities and women are accepted as reality. It is difficult for a librarian or teacher to convince children to question society's attitudes. But if a child can be shown how to detect racism and sexism in a book, the child can proceed to transfer the perception to wider areas. The following ten guidelines are offered as a starting point in evaluating children's books from this perspective.

1. Check the Illustrations

- *Look for stereotypes.* A stereotype is an oversimplified generalization about a particular group, race, or sex, which usually carries derogatory implications. Some infamous (overt) stereotypes of Blacks are the happy-go-lucky watermelon-eating Sambo and the fat, eye-rolling "mammy"; of Chicanos, the sombrero-wearing peon or fiesta-loving, macho bandito; of Asian Americans, the inscrutable, slant-eyed "Oriental"; of Native Americans, the naked savage or "primitive" craftsman and his squaw; of Puerto Ricans, the switchblade-toting teenage gang member; of women, the completely domesticated mother, the demure, doll-loving little girl, or the wicked stepmother. While you may not always find stereotypes in the blatant forms described, look for variations which in any way demean or ridicule characters because of their race or sex.

- *Look for tokenism.* If there are non-White characters in the illustrations, do they look just like Whites except for being tinted or colored in? Do all minority faces look stereotypically alike, or are they depicted as genuine individuals with distinctive features?

- *Who's doing what?* Do the illustrations depict minorities in subservient and passive roles or in leadership and action roles? Are males the active "doers" and females the inactive observers?

2. Check the Story Line

The Civil Rights Movement has led publishers to weed out many insulting passages, particularly from stories with Black themes, but the attitudes still find expression in less obvious ways. The following checklist suggests some of the subtle (covert) forms of bias to watch for.

- *Standard for success.* Does it take "White" behavior standards for a minority person to "get ahead"? Is "making it" in the dominant White society projected as the only ideal? To gain acceptance and approval, do non-White persons have to exhibit extraordinary qualities—excel in sports, get A's, etc.? In friendships between White and non-White children, is it the non-White who does most of the understanding and forgiving?

- *Resolution of problems.* How are problems presented, conceived, and resolved in the story? Are minority people considered to be "the problem"? Are the oppressions faced by minorities and women represented as causally related to an unjust society? Are the reasons for poverty and oppression explained, or are they accepted as inevitable? Does the story line encourage passive acceptance or active resistance? Is a particular problem that is faced by a minority person resolved through the benevolent intervention of a White person?

- *Role of women.* Are the achievements of girls and women based on their own initiative and intelligence, or are they due to their

Ten Quick Ways

good looks or to their relationship with boys? Are sex roles incidental or critical to characterization and plot? Could the same story be told if the sex roles were reversed?

3. Look at the Lifestyles

Are minority persons and their setting depicted in such a way that they contrast unfavorably with the unstated norm of White middle-class suburbia? If the minority group in question is depicted as "different," are negative value judgments implied? Are minorities depicted exclusively in ghettos, barrios, or migrant camps? If the illustrations and text attempt to depict another culture, do they go beyond oversimplifications and offer genuine insights into another lifestyle? Look for inaccuracy and inappropriateness in the depiction of other cultures. Watch for instances of the "quaint-natives-in-costume" syndrome (most noticeable in areas like costume and custom, but extending to behavior and personality traits as well).

4. Weigh the Relationships Between People

Do the Whites in the story possess the power, take the leadership, and make the important decisions? Do non-Whites and females function in essentially supporting roles?

How are family relationships depicted? In Black families, is the mother always dominant? In Hispanic families, are there always lots and lots of children? If the family is separated, are societal conditions—unemployment, poverty—cited among the reasons for the separation?

5. Note the Heroes and Heroines

For many years, books showed only "safe" minority heroes and heroines—those who avoided serious conflict with the White establishment of their time. Minority groups today are insisting on the right to define their own heroes and heroines based on their own concepts and struggles for justice.

When minority heroes and heroines do appear, are they admired for the same qualities that have made White heroes and heroines famous or because what they have done has benefitted White people? Ask this question: Whose interest is a particular figure really serving?

6. Consider the Effects on a Child's Self-Image

• *Are norms established that limit the child's aspirations and self-concepts?* What effect can it have on Black children to be continuously bombarded with images of the color white as the ultimate in beauty, cleanliness, virtue, etc., and the color black as evil, dirty, menacing, etc.? Does the book counteract or reinforce this positive association with the color white and negative association with black?

What happens to a girl's self-image when she reads that boys perform all of the brave and important deeds? What about a girl's self-esteem if she is not "fair" of skin and slim of body?

In a particular story, is there one or more persons with whom a minority child can readily identify to a positive and constructive end?

7. Consider the Author's or Illustrator's Background

Analyze the biographical material on the jacket flap or the back of the book. If a story deals with a minority theme, what qualifies the author or illustrator to deal with the subject? If the author and illustrator are not members of the minority being written about, is there anything in their background that would specifically recommend them as the creators of this book?

Similarly, a book that deals with the feelings and insights of women should be more carefully examined if it is written by a man —unless the book's avowed purpose is to present a strictly male perspective.

8. Check Out the Author's Perspective

No author can be wholly objective. All authors write out of a cultural as well as a personal context. Children's books in the past have traditionally come from authors who are White and who are members of the middle class, with one result being that a single ethnocentric perspective has dominated American children's literature. With the book in question, look carefully to determine whether the direction of the author's perspective substantially weakens or strengthens the value of his/her written work. Are omissions and distortions central to the overall character or "message" of the book?

9. Watch for Loaded Words

A word is loaded when it has insulting overtones. Examples of loaded adjectives (usually racist) are savage, primitive, conniving, lazy, superstitious, treacherous, wily, crafty, inscrutable, docile, and backward.

Look for sexist language and adjectives that exclude or ridicule women. Look for use of the male pronoun to refer to both males and females. While the generic use of the word "man" was accepted in the past, its use today is outmoded. The following examples show how sexist language can be avoided: ancestors instead of forefathers; chairperson instead of chairman; community instead of brotherhood; firefighters instead of firemen; manufactured instead of manmade; the human family instead of the family of man.

10. Look at the Copyright Date

Books on minority themes—usually hastily conceived—suddenly began appearing in the mid-1960s. There followed a growing number of "minority experience" books to meet the new market demand, but most of these were still written by White authors, edited by White editors, and published by White publishers. They therefore reflected a White point of view. Only very recently in the late 1960s and early 1970s, has the children's book world begun to even remotely reflect the realities of a multiracial society. And it has just begun to reflect feminists' concerns.

The copyright dates, therefore, can be a clue as to how likely the book is to be overtly racist or sexist, although a recent copyright date, of course, is no guarantee of a book's relevance or sensitivity. The copyright date only means the year the book was published. It usually takes a minimum of one year—and often much more than that—from the time a manuscript is submitted to the publisher to the time it is actually printed and put on the market. This time lag meant very little in the past, but in a time of rapid change and changing consciousness, when children's book publishing is attempting to be "relevant," it is becoming increasingly significant.

* * *

Reprinted with permission from the Council on Interracial Books for Children, Inc., 1841 Broadway, New York, NY 10023. Copies are available from the Council at 10¢ each plus a self-addressed, stamped envelope. The Council also publishes the *Bulletin* (eight issues a year), which reviews new children's books for the human and antihuman messages they convey.

Asian Americans

Books for Children

Anderson, Juanita B. **Charley Yee's New Year.** Follett, 1970. P

>Depicts San Francisco's Chinatown as Charley tries to follow the Chinese custom of repaying all debts by the new year.

Anno, Mitsumasa. **Anno's Alphabet: An Adventure in Imagination.** Crowell, 1975. NK

>This Japanese artist entices the reader with numerous uses of an object or letter—creative adventure.

Atwood, Ann. **Haiku: The Mood of the Earth.** Scribner's, 1971. KPA

>Words and photographs offer an experience in appreciation of nature. Young children can browse through color photographs.

Baron, Virginia Olsen, ed. **The Seasons of Time: Tanka Poetry of Ancient Japan.** Dial, 1968. KP

>The ancient Japanese concept of nature is revealed in this collection of poems. Coupled with black/gray/white ink and brush drawings, these poems are selected from the Manyoshu Collection. The ancient art forms reveal a contemporary sound.

Baron, Virginia Olsen. **Sunset in a Spider Web: Sijo Poetry of Ancient Korea.** Holt, Rinehart, and Winston, 1974. KPA

>Translations of Korean poetry offer insights into the culture. Poems and illustrations by Minja Kim involve children. Sijo poems have numerous syllables and are easier than haiku for young children to create.

Batterby, Michael. **Chinese and Oriental Art.** McGraw-Hill, 1961. KP

>A book for browsing. Text for older children. Handsome photographs of prints and Chinese art forms.

Behn, Harry. **More Cricket Songs.** Harcourt Brace Jovanovich, 1971. KP

>Japanese haiku translated from works of twenty-nine poets; some are illustrated with paintings by Japanese masters. Reading haiku often leads to children's writing and illustrating their own haiku.

Bryant, Sara Cone. **The Burning Rice Fields.** Holt, Rinehart, and Winston, 1963. KP

>The old ones are the wise ones. Delightful adventure with surprise ending. Appealing illustrations by Mamoru Funari.

Buck, Pearl S. **The Chinese Story Teller.** Day, 1971. NKP

>Despite the criticism that Buck is writing about a society with which she is not naturally affiliated, she gives us a rewarding experience. Colorfully illustrated pages are saturated with Chinese symbols.

Bulla, Clyde Robert. **Johnny Hong of Chinatown.** Crowell, 1952. P

>Setting is a United States Chinatown. Promotes understanding between ethnic groups.

Asian Americans

Cassidy, Sylvia, and K. Suetake. **Birds, Frogs, and Moonlight.** Doubleday, 1967. KP

    Calligraphy, watercolor illustrations by Vo-Dinh, and haiku provide an experience in the beauty of sound. "Notes on Haiku" is especially helpful in directing children's creation of haiku.

Copeland, Helen. **Meet Miki Takino.** Lothrop, Lee & Shepard, 1963. KP

    Miki, a Japanese-American boy, searches for grandparents to attend his school play. Stereotypes occupations and personalities of Japanese Americans.

Coutant, Helen. **First Snow.** Knopf, 1974. P

    A Vietnamese-American girl searches for the meaning of death. Provides few insights into Vietnamese-American life, but drawings and text portray warmth and sensitivity.

Evans, Doris Portwood. **Mr. Charley's Chopsticks.** Coward, McCann & Geoghegan, 1972. KP

    Involved tale of uses for Mr. Charley's chopsticks. Chinese culture is woven into a story for young children. Mother is depicted as a servant.

Flack, Marjorie, and K. Weise. **The Story about Ping.** Viking, 1933; renewed 1961. NK

    This popular story of Ping's adventures on the Yangtze River encourages children's dramatic play. However, its portrayal of physical punishment and stereotyping of Chinese with pigtails and traditional dress are untenable. Available in 16 mm film from Weston Woods.

Glubok, Shirley. **The Art of China.** Macmillan, 1973. KP

    A survey of art with photographs for young readers.

Glubok, Shirley. **The Art of Japan.** Macmillan, 1970. KP

    An introduction to Japanese painting, sculpture, flower arrangements, and gardens. Suggests painting a great wave similar to that of Kokusai.

Hawkinson, Lucy. **Dance Dance, Amy-Chan!** Whitman, 1964. KP

    A Japanese family tries to preserve traditions by sharing them with their Japanese-American children. The warm and loving relationship between the children and grandparents is a good model, but the book suffers from ageism and racism.

Hirawa, Yasuko. **Song of the Sour Plum: And Other Japanese Children's Songs.** Walker, 1968. K

    Printed first in Japan, the songs have been translated and written in poetic form. Illustrations are bright and startling. Few images of current Japanese culture.

Ishii, Momoko. **Issun Boshi: The Inchling.** Walker, 1965. KP

    Folktale of Japan. Fuku Akino's watercolor paintings enhance the story of a boy who is no bigger than a thumb. Another drama possibility.

Issa, Yayu, Kikaku, and other Japanese poets. **Don't Tell the Scarecrow and Other Japanese Poems.** Four Winds, 1969. KP

    Haiku may be read to interested children who cannot read. The poems relate to specific seasons. Some children may wish to dictate or write haiku after hearing Issa's haiku.

Iwasaki, Chikiro. **Will You Be My Friend.** McGraw-Hill, 1973. KP

    Japanese author relates a tale about understanding between persons and deals with the subject through children. The story loses impact because of translation. Charcoal drawings dominate the text. Other books by Iwasaki that children enjoy are *A New Baby Is Coming* and *The Birthday Wish*.

Books for Children

Jaynes, Ruth. **Friends, Friends, Friends.** Bowman, 1967. P

    An Asian-American girl is depicted within a school setting. Unfortunately, all but one of the professional adults are Caucasian.

Kimishima, Hisako. **The Princess of the Rice Fields.** Weatherhill, 1970. KP

    Demons, a princess, and transformation—exciting themes for young children. The Indonesian folktale is illustrated by Sumiko Muzushi. Children ask to see the illustrations of demons and gods again and again.

Krueger, Kermit. **The Golden Swans.** World, 1969. KP

    This Thai folktale embodies Buddhist and Hindu doctrines in telling the famous legend from the Mekhong plateau area of the Statue of the Swans. The story deals with the premise that even though we cannot change some things we can find ways to make them bearable. Chinese-American artist Ed Young presents watercolor collage.

Lewis, Richard, ed. **There Are Two Lives: Poems by Children of Japan.** Simon and Schuster, 1970. KP

    Respect for the arts is depicted in this collection. Children identify with poems such as "A Song of Wetting the Bed," "Daddy in the Dream," and "When I Read My Poems."

Lewis, Thomas P. **The Dragon Kite.** Holt, Rinehart and Winston, 1974. KP

    Relates the story of Kesang's journey in search of the Great Dragon. Young children delight in colorful illustrations of the Great Dragon with "wings like clouds and eyes like two red suns."

Matsuno, Masako. **A Pair of Red Clogs.** World, 1960. KP

    Reminiscing about grandmother's beautiful tale of red clogs and being young allows children to identify with the feeling of having new shoes and their commitment to them. Deals with accepting one's own poor judgments and learning from them.

Matsuno, Masako. **Taro and the Bamboo Shoot.** Pantheon, 1964. KP

    Villagers' lives are enhanced because of a young boy's adventures in a bamboo grove. Japanese folktale that is excellent for dramatizing. Yasuo Segawa's illustrations increase interest in the tale.

Matsutani, Miyoko. **The Crane Maiden.** Parents' Magazine Press, 1968. KP

    In this English version of the Japanese folktale "Tsuru No Ongaeshi," an old man's kind deed is repaid. Children can dramatize this story.

McDermott, Gerald. **The Stonecutter: A Japanese Folk Tale.** Viking, 1975. KP

    Japanese folklore is interpreted graphically and in vivid color by an author who illustrates films and books for children. Theme of the myth is the foolish longing for power. Available in 16mm film from Weston Woods.

Mizumura, Kazue. **I See the Winds.** Crowell, 1966. NK

    The Japanese author uses watercolor illustrations to complement the poems.

Mosel, Arlene. **Tikki Tikki Temo.** Holt, Rinehart and Winston, 1968. NKP

    Young children are the wise ones in this humorous tale about why Chinese names are short. Available in 16mm film from Weston Woods.

Niizaka, Kazuo. **Clouds.** Addison-Wesley, 1975. K

    Japanese artist of numerous children's books reflects on clouds through poetic text and clear paintings.

Otsuha, Yuzo. **Suko and the White Horse: A Legend of Mongolia.** Bobbs-Merrill, 1967. KP

   Beautiful tale of Suko's love for the White Horse. The tale tells how the horsehead fiddle became an instrument preferred by Asians. Pleasing watercolor illustrations.

Phillips, Barbara. **Nok Noy and the Charcoal Man.** Addison-Wesley, 1970. KP

   Nok Noy's appetite for rice takes the reader on an adventure through the busy, enormous city. Illustrations by Sylvie Selig capture the culture of Thailand, with boiled rice and spice for breakfast, the clattering coal wagon, sweet-smelling papayas in brimming baskets swaying from a pole, a sweet coffee and tea vendor, banana trees, a Sikh selling colored beads, and a fried noodle vendor.

Robertson, Dorothy Lewis, retold. **Fairy Tales from Viet Nam.** Dodd, Mead, 1968. KP

   Text should be selectively read or told to young children. Includes stories of talking animals and magic.

Sarasas, Claude. **The ABC's of Origami: Paper Folding for Children.** Tuttle, 1964. KPA

   Origami projects made simple through descriptive diagrams and illustrations. Some young children engage in this activity without difficulty.

Soong, Maying. **The Art of Chinese Paper Folding: For Young and Old.** Harcourt Brace Jovanovich, 1948. KPA

   Clear instructions and simple diagrams.

Sternberg, Martha. **Japan: A Week in Daisuke's World.** Macmillan, 1973. KP

   The Araki family involves young children in both modern and traditional Japan. Full-page photographs by Minoru Aoki dominate the experience. Through the eyes of second-grader Daisuke, young children tour a department store, visit a candy seller, see Sumo wrestling, and view the cherry blossoms.

Titus, Eve. **The Two Stonecutters.** Doubleday, 1967. KP

   This is a tale of "wish spending." Yoko Mitsuhashi, a Japanese artist, adds to the tale with bold, vivid illustrations.

Wyndham, Robert. **Chinese Mother Goose Rhymes.** World, 1968. KP

   Translations of classic poems. These three-line expressions can be meaningful for young children as they create their own poems. Illustrations by Ed Young can be used by young children as a basis for Chinese writing.

Yashima, Mitsu, and T. Yashima. **Momo's Kitten.** Viking, 1961. NK

   Momo's experience with a kitten has value for young children who are making discoveries about growth and reproduction. No cultural insights—only the names are Japanese. Story by a sensitive and gifted author. Also available in cassette/eight paperbacks/teacher's guide from Baker & Taylor.

Yashima, Mitsu, and T. Yashima. **Plenty to Watch.** Viking, 1954. NK

   With meaningful dialog and crayon illustrations, this book substantiates the view that children's classrooms should be their world.

Yashima, Taro. **Crow Boy.** Viking, 1955. NK

   Yashima takes us on a search for valuable truths. Helps children see value in understanding the feelings of others. Available in 16mm film from Weston Woods.

Yashima, Taro. **Seashore Story.** Viking, 1967. NKP

   Young children at the seashore are reminded of an old familiar tale about Urashima, the fisherman who went on a journey to the bottom of the ocean and "stayed away too long." Unusual crayon illustrations.

Books for Children

Yashima, Taro. **Umbrella.** Viking, 1969. NK

Japanese-American Momo desires to use her new umbrella and boots. She learns patience and self-confidence in this sensitively written story.

Yashima, Taro. **The Village Tree.** Viking, 1953. KP

A tree for climbing, swinging, and seesawing; a chair, a house, a place for a snack or a game of "Bamboo-Hide." Activities that appeal to all children; one of Yashima's best books. Filmstrip/cassette available from Baker & Taylor.

Yashima, Taro. **Youngest One.** Viking, 1962. NK

Describes the feelings of an introverted two-year-old boy in brief text and pastels. One can sense the value of extended families. Children can learn about Japanese cultural values while experiencing the struggle to relate interpersonally.

Resources for Adults

Books and Articles

Asaki Origami Club. **Origami.** Chiyoda, 1959. Distributed by Japan Publishing Trading Co., Ltd.

    Some children can make animals or birds by folding paper.

Berger, Donald P. **Folk Songs of Japanese Children.** Tuttle, 1969.

    Representative songs that are familiar throughout Japan and in specific locales. The annotations provide background information for adults.

Buell, Hal. **Viet Nam: Land of Many Dragons.** Dodd, Mead, 1968.

    Excellent photographs of the Vietnamese people engaged in planting and cultivation of rice and fishing in Mekong Delta's marshland.

Contrasts and Conflicts: The Asian Immigration Experience. Asian American Studies Center, 1975.

    Discusses effects of immigration on history and today's Asian Americans.

Counterpoint: Perspectives on Asian America. Asian American Studies Center, 1977.

    Anthology of Asian American research studies and writing that challenges conventional writing of the past one hundred years. Includes areas of labor, history, race, class, women, education, and immigration.

Dowdell, Dorothy, and J. Dowdell. **The Chinese Helped Build America.** Messner, 1972.

    This simply written book glosses over the realities of Chinese Americans who have suffered from oppression, racism, and paternalism.

Dowdell, Dorothy, and J. Dowdell. **The Japanese Helped Build America.** Messner, 1970.

    Again, superficial and inaccurate treatment of the historical background and lives of Japanese Americans.

Houn, Florence, and T. Lee. **Multicultural Workshop Resource Packet on Asian Americans.** Amherst Asian American Committee.

    Book is a thrust to facilitate the development of multicultural education and "abolish the policy of educational neglect concerning Asian American studies." Supplies historical background of Japanese-American experience. Annotated bibliography of materials.

Inui, Lloyd, and F. Odo. **Asian American Experience.** California State University Asian Studies Department, 1974.

    Written for teachers. Provides basic information and issues regarding Chinese, Japanese, Filipino, Korean, and Pacific Islander communities. Includes guide to audiovisual materials.

Resources for Adults

McCarry, Charles. **Kyoto and Nara: Keepers of Japan's Past.** *National Geographic* 149 (June 1976): 836-851. National Geographic Society.

"If the impulse to equal the old master ever dies among the new generations of our artists, then Japan will lose part of her spirit." Kyoto, a city housing many national treasures and artifacts, strives to live and work tuned to Japan's cultural history, recreating traditional styles. Color photographs reveal traditional dances, painters, sculptors, actors, game enthusiasts, and musicians.

Melendy, Howard B. **The Oriental Americans.** Twayne, 1972.

A survey of Chinese and Japanese immigration to America. These Asian immigrants and their descendants have enriched our cultural heritage.

Miller, Richard J., and L. Katoh. **Japan.** Watts, 1969.

Special art section with photographs of bonsai and flower arrangements. Photographs of students printing symbols.

White, Florence, and K. Akiyama. **Children's Songs from Japan.** Marks Music Corporation, 1960.

The authors have captured the spirit of the children of Japan in this collection of folk and other songs from Japan. Authentic illustrations by Toshihiko Suzuki. The explanations and phonetic pronunciations aid in appreciating Japanese words and music.

14 Bibliographies

A Bibliography of Asian and Asian-American Books for Elementary School Youngsters. Sponsored by Asian American Cultural Heritage Program and Asian American Education Association. Distributed by Office of State Superintendent of Public Instruction.

An extensive annotated list of books and resources for teaching.

The Chinese in Children's Books. New York Public Library, 1974.

A selected annotated list of English and Chinese books about the Chinese. Includes a section on "The Chinese in the United States."

Getting to Know China Through Books (K-9): An Annotated Bibliography of Children's Books. Stanford Area Chinese Club, Service-Cultural Committee.

Juana Dong compiled extensive list of resources pertaining to Chinese culture.

The Japanese and the Japanese Americans. Association of Children's Librarians.

A fifteen-page bibliography of educational materials for children.

Japanese Children's Books. New York Public Library.

Request catalog. Lists Japanese books with brief descriptions and includes American publisher, if available.

Catalogs

China Books and Periodicals.

Foreign Language Press, publications. Resources depict current Chinese values and ideals.

Chinese Bilingual Pilot Project. San Francisco Unified School District, ESEA Title VII.

This project has produced a number of illustrated story booklets in Chinese and English—"Winter Festival," "The Story of Ching Ming," "The Moon Festival Is Here," and "Preparing for Chinese New Year"—and some information pamphlets—"Background Materials on Ching Ming Festival" and "Chinese New Year Resource Material."

Chinese Information Service.

Request information on subscriptions for journals and other publications.

Japanese American Curriculum Project.

Distributes a wide range of materials, from a Japanese-English ABC picture book through university journals and adult materials.

Selector's Guide for Bilingual Educational Materials. Vol. 3. EPIE Institute, 1976.

Programs in Chinese, Japanese, Korean, and Vietnamese. Reports on Asian materials development and instructional design. Guidelines for selecting materials and addresses of sources of instructional materials. EPIE Institute compiled this volume of Asian bilingual instructional materials to assist in selecting appropriate materials.

Sino-American Cultural Society.

Conducts discussion groups, lectures, courses of study, and other programs. Encourages performance of the arts. Pamphlets and other publications available.

Charles E. Tuttle Co.

Publishes books about Asian-American cultures.

Periodicals

BABEL. Bay Area Bilingual Education League of the Berkeley, California, United School District Bilingual Project.

Publishes a newsletter and a catalog of materials produced by BABEL.

Focus on Asian Studies. Service Center for Teachers of Asian Studies.

A newsletter for teachers. Includes book reviews and announcements of conferences, publications, multimedia materials, and summer programs.

Japan. Ministry of Foreign Affairs, Japan. Distributed by Japan National Tourist Organization.

Magazine published quarterly in Japan illustrates in large colorful photographs the developments in Japan, the interests of modern Japan, and a glimpse of the traditional. Printed in English.

Materials and Experiences

Posters/Pictures

Embassy of Japan.
> Source for information and posters.

Embassy of the Republic of China.
> Source for information and posters.

Filipino Youth Activities of Seattle.
> Write for information on a variety of available teaching aids.

Mainland China—Today. Cook, 1973. Distributed by School Products Division.
> Sixteen 12½" x 17" pictures and a teacher's manual presenting Chinese culture. Depicts leaders, crafts, people, folktales, art, music, and family life. Authentic illustrations. Order #68528.

Royal Thai Embassy.
> Source for information and posters.

Tourist and Travel Offices—Posters and pictures available.
> China Airlines, Ltd.
> Japan Air Lines.
> Japan National Tourist Organization.
> Republic of China Tourism Bureau.

Records

Chi Chi Pa Pa, with Margaret Marks. *Making Music Your Own.* Six-record album. Produced by Silver Burdett. Distributed by General Learning Corporation, Album #75180.
> Have you ever heard about a school for birds? This song tells about one.

Empress of the Pagodas. *Making Music Your Own.* Six-record album. Produced by Silver Burdett. Distributed by General Learning Corporation. Album #75180.
> Music for listening. Children create and dramatize stories.

A Grain of Sand, by Chris Iijima, Nobuko Miyamoto, and Charlie Chin. Produced and distributed by Paredon Records.
> Original music from the late 1960s and early 1970s.

Japanese Rain Song, with Roberta McLaughlin. *Making Music Your Own.* Six-record album. Produced by Silver Burdett. Distributed by General Learning Corporation. Album #75180.
> A rainy day in Japan prompts gestures and movement.

Films/Filmstrips

Festival in Japan. American-English version. Produced by Sakura Motion Picture Co. Distributed by Japan National Tourist Organization, Dallas, Texas.

Festivals in Japan. Film #67, 21 minutes.

Japan in Winter. American-English version. Produced by Sakura Motion Picture Co. Distributed by Japan National Tourist Organization, Dallas, Texas.

Scenes with birds migrating, kites flying, farming, fishing, and ice skating. Entertaining for young children. Film #46, 17 minutes.

Just Like Me. Oakland Unified School District.

Animated film about the value of being an individual.

Toymaker. Oakland Unified School District.

Depicts the many ways in which all people are alike.

Slides

Travel Slides. Produced by Technicolor Corporation. Distributed by Slides Unlimited.

Request a catalog of slides.

Museums

China Institute in America.

Founded to introduce Americans to Chinese cultures and to improve community relations. Maintains a library and a gallery of Chinese art.

Japan House Gallery.

Features guided tours, lectures, films, concerts, dance recitals, drama, and arts festivals.

Festivals/Fairs/Celebrations

Aki Matsure (Fall Festival). Japan Center, San Francisco. Held in late September. Contact San Francisco Chamber of Commerce.

Cherry Blossom Festival. Japan Center, Nihonmachi, San Francisco. Held in late April. Contact San Francisco Convention and Visitors Bureau.

Chinese New Year. Celebrated in the following locations:

Chinatown, Boston, Massachusetts. Contact Greater Boston Chamber of Commerce.
Chinatown, Chicago, Illinois. Contact Chicago Convention and Tourism Bureau.
Chinatown, New York, New York. Contact New York Convention and Visitors Bureau.
Chinatown, Philadelphia, Pennsylvania. Contact Philadelphia Convention and Visitors Bureau.
Chinatown, San Francisco, California. Contact San Francisco Convention and Visitors Bureau.
Chinatown, Washington, D.C. Contact Washington Area Convention and Visitors Association.

Japanese Tea Ceremony. Japanese Gardens, Botanical Gardens, Birmingham, Alabama. Held in mid-June. Contact Alabama Bureau of Publicity and Information.

Nisei Week. Little Tokyo, Los Angeles, California. Held in mid-August. Contact Southern California Visitors Council.

Black Americans

Books for Children

Aardema, Verna, retold. **Behind the Back of the Mountain: Black Folktales from Southern Africa.** Dial, 1973. KP

"A hundred years ago the story teller, Hiddora Kabbo, said that when one has traveled along a road, he can sit down and wait for a story to overtake him. He said a story is like the wind. It comes from a far place and it can pass behind the back of a mountain." Illustrations are by Leo and Diane Dillon.

Aardema, Verna, retold. **Why Mosquitoes Buzz in Peoples' Ears.** Dial, 1975. KP

This West African tale about a disaster caused when Mosquito tells Iguana a "tall tale" is cleverly retold by Aardema and brilliantly illustrated by Leo and Diane Dillon. Ideal for dramatizing, it offers a total artistic experience. African inspired designs reveal numerous shapes, images, and color blends. Watercolor/airbrush illustrations help to enrich the magical quality of the tale. This book received the Caldecott Medal in 1976. Aardema has also retold African folktales in *Otwe*, *The Na of Wa*, and *Tales from the Story Hat*, but unappealing illustrations limit the value of these books.

Adoff, Arnold, ed. **Black Out Loud: An Anthology of Modern Poems by Black Americans.** Macmillan, 1970. KP

This anthology of poems conveys Black pride. Brave poets such as Langston Hughes, Le Roi Jones, Nikki Giovanni, and Gwendolyn Brooks are included. Be selective of poems to read to young children. Some appealing sketches by Alvin Hillingsworth.

Adoff, Arnold. **MA nDA LA.** Harper & Row, 1971. KP

Rhyming syllables and colorful full-page illustrations explore the lifestyle of one African family.

Adoff, Arnold, ed. **My Black Me: A Beginning Book of Black Poetry.** Dutton, 1975. KP

Representative of the thoughts and feelings of twenty-five poets, including Nikki Giovanni and Langston Hughes. They deal with what it means to be Black in a meaningful, authentic way.

Alexander, Martha. **The Story Grandmother Told.** Dial, 1969. NKP

Pleasing illustrations depict a meaningful, relaxed relationship between a grandmother and child. Grandmother is stereotyped in apron and cooking in every scene, but she does set work aside to play with the child.

Alkema, Chester J. **Masks.** Sterling, 1971. NKP

Provide this vividly illustrated book when children want to be animals or perhaps a "do do" spirit. The child may use the directions for making a mask or the book may stimulate the child's own creations.

Allen, William D. **Africa.** Fideler, 1974. KP

Photographs of shoppers at the market in Ivory Coast, sunbathers on the beach at Cape Town, Kano homes and modern city dwellings in Casablanca. Old and new ways are explored in detailed text for older children and adults. This is a typical geography book. Photos can be used with young children; text is for upper-elementary children. Photos expose the segregation except for Moslem schools. Text focuses on problems, states, "The black people are *not* given equal rights with the whites."

Arnatt, Kathleen. **African Myths and Legends.** Walck, 1967. KPA

"Tale of the Super Man," "The Rubber Man," and "The Monkey's Heart" are among the favorites in this collection of folktales representing numerous African nations. Adult text can be adapted for young children.

Baldwin, Anne N. **Sunflowers for Tina.** Four Winds, 1970. KP

Tina's desire to "grow something" finds expression as she views two stalks of flowers bursting from ruins of a broken building. Bold colors and descriptive text positively portray a sensitive Black child's feelings about life and death.

Breinburg, Petronella. **Dr. Shawn.** Crowell, 1975. NK

The attractive crayon illustrations by Errol Lloyd add a dimension to the story of children playing "hospital," which points out that girls may also choose to become doctors. Children read this story over and over.

Breinburg, Petronella. **Shawn Goes to School.** Crowell, 1973. NK

Children identify with Shawn's first day at school. "Shawn didn't seem to like it much" is dramatized in full-page crayon drawings with an easy-to-read text. The Black author portrays a Black child as the main protagonist in an integrated environment.

Burch, Robert. **Joey's Cat.** Viking, 1969. KP

Children can identify with Joey's preoccupation with a cat and his mother's reluctance to keep it. Muted colors complement the text.

Caines, Jeannette F. **Abby.** Harper & Row, 1973. KP

Dealing with adoption is commendable and this book helps to fill the void of material focusing on the subject. However, the illustrations and dialog are undesirable in terms of building respect for Black culture.

Carpenter, John A., and T. Balow. **Enchantment of Africa: Botswana.** Children's Press, 1973. KP

The story of this southern country in Africa describes people and their lifestyles. Photos of children in school, people working, and animals used as means of transportation.

Carpenter, John A., and M. De Lang. **Enchantment of Africa: Kenya.** Children's Press, 1973. KP

One in a series of enchantment books about the culture of Kenya. Section on animals with vivid photos and Swahili words.

Church, Vivian. **Colors Around Me.** Afro-American Publishing, 1971. NK

Beauty of skin colors is explored, and the book equates color of food with skin color of children. May have negative effect if child is sensitive to references made to her or his skin.

Clifton, Lucille. **The Boy Who Didn't Believe in Spring.** Dutton, 1973. NK

King Shabazz is encouraged by his friends and family to believe that spring is coming. Tony Polito, also skeptic, joins him on an adventure to find spring. The author has captured Black-American dialect and depicts an integrated school and community with Black majority. Also available in Spanish.

Books for Children

Clifton, Lucille. **Don't You Remember?** Dutton, 1973. NK

Two famous Black artists (Evaline Ness is illustrator) collaborate on this adventure of a four-year-old who forgets her own birthday. The book portrays a positive Black family image.

Clifton, Lucille. **Good, Says Jerome.** Dutton, 1973. NK

Imaginative venture by two Black artists deals with fears of young children. Stephanie Douglas's bright collages add quality to the book.

Clifton, Lucille. **Some of the Days of Everett Anderson.** Holt, Rinehart and Winston, 1970. NK

All of Everett's days in an urban setting are interesting to other six-year-olds. Illustrations by Evaline Ness complement the mood and portrayal of a Black child's thoughts and feelings. However, the "Wednesday Noon Adventure" stereotypes Native Americans.

Cornish, Sam. **Grandmother's Pictures.** Bradbury, 1974. KP

An impressionable narrative of a young boy's relationship with his Grandmother Keyes. Her accounts of his family documented in a scrapbook allow him a glimpse of his father, Grandmother Nickols, Miss Carrol, friends of his mother, and "house" pictures. The charcoal sketches by Jeanne Johns assist in the relating of a major Black poet's experience.

Crippen, David. **Two Sides of the River.** Abingdon, 1976. KP

The Kenyan families of Makokha and Otaka have been enemies since the days of their grandfathers. While tending the cows, Otaka is caught in a swift current.

D'Amato, Alex, and J. D'Amato. **African Animals Through African Eyes.** Messner, 1971. NKP

Illustrations from original art forms in museum and text give clues about African animals.

D'Amato, Alex, and J. D'Amato. **African Crafts for You to Make.** Messner, 1970. NKP

Explicit directions on how to make replicas of chad houses, tie-dye fabrics, and a simplified version of the game "manhala." Interests children in crafts as well as involving them in African cultural experiences.

Dayrell, Elphinstone. **Why the Sun and the Moon Live in the Sky.** Houghton Mifflin, 1968. KP

An Efjik-bibio folktale about the origin of the world. These people dressed to represent the elements and the creatures of the sea. Also available in Spanish and in filmstrip/cassette from ACI Films.

Desbarats, Peter. **Gabriella and Selena.** Harcourt Brace Jovanovich, 1968. KP

Illustrated in charcoal drawings, the story reveals a positive relationship between a Black child and a White child.

Dietz, Betty W., A. Babatunde, and M. Babatunde. **Musical Instruments of Africa.** Day, 1965. KP

Book familiarizes children with numerous musical instruments used in Africa, and points out how African music has inspired music in America. Good ideas for making instruments with available materials. Record accompanying book is enjoyable.

Doob, Leonard W., ed. **A Crocodile Has Me by the Leg: African Poems.** Walker, 1966. KP

African poems illustrated in woodcuts by Nigerian artist Irein Wangboje. Introduces young children to a broad view of life in Africa. "Dance of the Animals" lends itself to dance and movement interpretations. "We Mold a Pot as Our Mothers Did" relates technique and appreciation for cultural heritage.

Dorbin, Arnold. **Josephine's 'Magination: A Tale of Haiti.** Four Winds, 1973. KP

Clothing, foods, homes, and indications of French influence enrich this story about a young girl who uses her creative ability to satisfy her desire for a doll. Elaborate watercolor illustrations are used.

Ebony Pictorial History of Black America. 4 vols. Johnson, 1971, 1974. NKP

Begins with the African past and continues through 1973. Photographs and illustrations by artists interpret the text.

Feelings, Muriel. **Jambo Means Hello.** Dial, 1974. NK

Swahili alphabet book teaches language and gives cultural information.

Feelings, Muriel. **Moja Means One: Swahili Counting Book.** Dial, 1971. NK

Brief text takes reader from one to ten in Swahili while describing East African culture. Descriptive illustrations of market stalls, mothers, instruments, manhala, and coffee trees interest children. Learning another language can lead to better understanding of any culture.

Fife, Dale. **Adam's ABC.** Coward, McCann & Geoghegan, 1971. NK

Alphabet book focuses on urban setting. Charcoal drawings complement text.

Foster, F. Blanche. **Dahomey.** Watts, 1971. KP

Section on music can be used with *Rhythms of Childhood* record. Pictures of spirited dances and a display of drums are included.

Fraser, Kathleen, and M. F. Levy. **Adam's World: San Francisco.** Whitman, 1971. NK

Reflects pride in Black culture through importance placed on positive family relations. Full-page illustrations enable young children to view how one Black community lives.

Fufuka, Karama, and M. Fufuka. **My Daddy Is a Cool Dude and Other Poems.** Dial, 1975. KPA

Portraits of Tom, Big Mama, parades, Slick and Cool Dude Dad. Poems and sketches record authentic experiences in a Black community. Although the material is honest and does not skirt reality, an adult should select those poems appropriate for young children.

Giovanni, Nikki. **Spin a Soft Black Song: Poems for Children.** Hill and Wang, 1971. NK

This significant Black poet coupled with Charles Bible to "write a book of poems 'cause when we were growing up, there were precious few of them. Especially for us, and we wanted to say things the way we said things when we were little."

Graham, Lorenz. **Song of the Boat.** Crowell, 1975. NK

Adventure of Momolu's search for a canoe for his beloved father. The author's concern with authenticity is evident in his style and content; his poetic style reiterates a rhythm of the language used. Woodcuts are by Leo and Diane Dillon.

Gray, Genevieve. **Send Wendell.** McGraw-Hill, 1974. NK

This story about a young boy's role in the family portrays a positive Black image. The text is augmented by Symeon Shimin's beautiful illustrations.

Greenfield, Eloise. **First Pink Light.** Crowell, 1976. NKP

Tyree waits up for his father's return after caring for his ill mother. Soft charcoal illustrations enhance the warmth of the story.

Books for Children

Greenfield, Eloise. **Me and Nessie.** Crowell, 1975. NK

Young children identify with Janell's friendship with Nessie. Sensitive, understanding Black parents and Aunt Bea give depth to the story written in Black dialect.

Gross, Mary Ann, ed. **Ah, Man, You Found Me Again.** Beacon, 1972. KP

Numerous vignettes by minorities provide insight about the injustice of denying ghetto inhabitants their own language. "They should not have to forsake their roots in order to be accepted into middle-class life." Impressive portraits and stories are extemporaneous expressions of feelings and thoughts. Especially important is the understanding of originality of dialect and lifestyles.

Haley, Gail. **A Story A Story: An African Tale Retold.** Atheneum, 1970. NKP

Adventures of Ananse, the "Spider Man," as he outwits others in order to pay the price that Sky God wants for stories. Illustrations are geometric and in bold colors. Also available in film from Weston Woods.

Halmi, Robert. **Visit to a Chief's Son: An American Boy's Adventures with an African Tribe.** Holt, Rinehart and Winston, 1963. KP

"The more Dionni and Kevin worked and played together, the less strange they seemed to each other." These photographs and story about the Masai culture can be shared even with young children.

Hamilton, Virginia. **Time-Ago Lost: More Tales of Jahdu.** Macmillan, 1973. KP

Mama Luka fantasizes to the delight of Richard Lee. The text, for older children, can be interpreted by adults. Stories of magic are especially enjoyable to young children. The relationships and contemporary setting offer another level of appreciation.

Hamilton, Virginia. **The Time-Ago Tales of Jahdu.** Macmillan, 1969. KP

"In her tight little room in a fine, good place called Harlem," Mama Luka creates Jahdu adventures for her young friend Lee Edward. The relationship between the two is a good model for children. Illustrations by Nonny Hogrogian are in soft, subtle pencil sketches, and the author, granddaughter of a slave, involves us in a Black experience.

Hayes Story Reader of Young Black Americans. Afro-American Publishing, n.d. KP

Twenty-eight biographies dealing mostly with childhood incidents with which Black children can readily identify.

Hodges, Elizabeth J. **Free as a Frog.** Addison-Wesley, 1969. NK

An introverted six-year-old finds a frog and becomes an active member of his class and his family. Drawings by Paul Giovanopoulos portray a supportive and caring Black community.

Hopkins, Lee Bennett. **Don't You Turn Back: Poems by Langston Hughes.** Knopf, 1967. KP

This collection of poems was selected by young children for a poetry memorial. Hughes's poetry is often told in Black English, as in "Mother to Son." The rhythm of Black music is experienced in "Dream Variations." Woodcuts by Ann Grifalconi are exceptional.

Jones, Bessie, et al. **Step It Down.** Harper & Row, 1972. NKPA

With songs and games that are based on the developmental process of young children, this book moves from learning "how to clap" to sophisticated rhythm. *Step It Down* should be included when planning an awareness session on Black culture, because it is an excellent resource for involving young children in songs/games attributed to Black communities.

Jordan, June. **Who Look at Me.** Crowell, 1969. KPA

> Examines paintings of Black people. Poems illustrating the paintings are sensitive, descriptive, and add a new dimension to the aesthetic possibilities of the book. Adults should read every page, then select those to share with children!

Keats, Ezra Jack. **Goggles.** Macmillan, 1969. NK

> Adventure of three friends and their excitement and struggle over a pair of goggles. Delightful illustrations with a wealth of color and detail that capture the interest of children.

Keats, Ezra Jack. **Hi Cat.** Macmillan, 1970. NK

> What happens when Archie plans a show is a hilarious tale. Humorous illustrations add to the interest of the book.

Keats, Ezra Jack. **Peter's Chair.** Harper & Row, 1967. NK

> Peter struggles with himself to accept his baby sister as part of the family.

Keats, Ezra Jack. **The Snowy Day.** Viking, 1962. NK

> Adventures on a snowy day. Also available in cassette with eight-page teacher guide from Baker & Taylor.

Keats, Ezra Jack. **Whistle for Willie.** Macmillan, 1971. NK

> Learning to whistle can be difficult for a young boy. Film available from Weston Woods.

Klimowitz, Barbara. **When Shoes Eat Socks.** Abingdon, 1971. NK

> Children are amused with Barnaby as his "shoes eat socks." Learning to tie shoes can mean being accepted and given a turn as "Shadow Man."

Lester, Julius. **The Knee-High Man and Other Tales.** Dial, 1972. KP

> Black folk literature is related by a Black author from "the heritage of my people." Young children are fascinated by the adventure stories—some sad, some funny. This collection of folktales, with colorful detailed illustrations by Ralph Pinto, is an exceptional experience.

Lexau, Joan M. **Benjie.** Dial, 1964. NK

> "Then the terrible thing happened." And the terrible incident turned bashful Benjie into a boy who "hadn't let anybody stop him from finding the earring."

Lexau, Joan M. **Benjie on His Own.** Dial, 1970. NK

> Experience on Harlem streets when Benjie realizes Granny isn't coming to meet him. Again, author Lexau and illustrator Don Bolognese collaborate on a story about the isolation, poverty, and kindness that can exist together in a community.

Lexau, Joan M. **Me Day.** Dial, 1971. KP

> Rafu's birthday is special with cake for supper, first choice at television shows, no chores, and a surprise awaiting him at the fruit store by the bus stop. The lifestyle portrayed relates to the actual experiences of numerous children.

McDermott, Gerald. **Anansi, the Spider: A Tale from the Ashanti.** Holt, Rinehart and Winston, 1972. NKP

> This story from the long established culture of Ghana, has been passed on orally for many generations. Kwaku Anansi's adventures are illustrated in a combination of geometric forms and colors. The movement in design and interweaving of brilliant color and symbols is a rewarding and favorite experience for children. Also available in film and filmstrip/record from Weston Woods.

Books for Children

McGovern, Ann. **Black Is Beautiful.** Four Winds, 1972. NK

Booklet portrays positive Black imagery that is important for all children.

Mendoza, George. **And I Must Hurry for the Sea Is Coming In.** Prentice-Hall, 1969. Photographs by DeWayne Dalrymple. NKP

Black child dreams of the sea. The brief poem is a meaningful companion to this selection of photographs.

Rinkoff, Barbara. **Rutherford T. Finds 21 B.** Putnam's, 1970. KP

It was the first day of school and Rutherford needed a friend. Children will identify with his fear of loneliness.

Roberts, Nancy. **A Week in Robert's World: The South.** Macmillan, 1969. NK

Young children are attracted to books dominated by illustrations or photographs. Robert Lee's world is a supporting, caring, and interesting one.

Savory, Phyllis. **Lion Outwitted by Hare and Other African Tales.** Whitman, 1971. KP

The author grew up on a farm in Rhodesia and relates tales reminiscent of folklore from many lands. Adults should choose those tales to be told to children.

Schatz, Letta. **Banji's Magic Wheel.** Follett, 1975. NK

A teacher of young children in Nigeria spins a tale about growing up in a West African village. Woodcuts by Ann Grifalconi illustrate an adventure with which young children can identify.

Scott, Ann H. **Sam.** McGraw-Hill, 1967. NK

Sam is lonely and needs someone in his family. The family members are occupied with various activities until Sam cries to make his need known. Appealing illustrations of a Black family by Symeon Shimin.

Seed, Jenny. **Kulumi the Brave: A Zulu Tale.** World, 1970. KP

Authentic folktale related by a woman who lives in Africa. Insertion of Zulu language in this adventure of Kulumi with dramatic full-color illustrations provides a rewarding experience for children.

Steptoe, John. **Birthday.** Holt, Rinehart and Winston, 1972. NK

Friends and family in Yowba celebrate Javuka's eighth birthday. Realistic language is used.

Steptoe, John. **Stevie.** Harper & Row, 1969. NK

Excellent insight about how a child feels when he is confronted with sharing toys, his mother, and urban home.

Stone, Elberta. **I'm Glad I'm Me.** Putnam's, 1971. NK

Black child reveals positive self-image. Charcoal sketches depict city environment and interaction with other Blacks.

Sutherland, Efua. **Playtime in Africa.** Atheneum, 1963. KP

"Come and share all the happy games we play." Games and recreational activities from Ghana are written in poetic form and appeal to young children.

Thomas, Ianthe. **Lordy Aunt Hattie.** Harper & Row, 1973. NK

"See the mornin' I done brought fo' you," the Black author writes to set the mood and feeling of early summertime. Quiet pictures and rhythmic text.

Udry, Janice M. **Mary Jo's Grandmother.** Whitman, 1972. KP

A visit to grandmother is complicated by an accident. Stereotyping of the grandmother is offensive, and situation is contrived.

Udry, Janice M. **What Mary Jo Shared.** Whitman, 1968. KP

This book is about a Black child as she strives to find something special to share at school.

Udry, Janice M. **What Mary Jo Wanted.** Whitman, 1968. KP

In this story of a Black family adjusting to a new pet, Mary Jo proves she can be responsible and solve problems.

Wagner, Jane. **J. T.** Miller-Brody, 1967. KP

Based on true life of a ghetto child in an integrated neighborhood; young children enjoy the excitement and adventure surrounding the "cat" episode. The book exhibits problems in these areas: (1) racism—a White man saves the day, (2) sexism—"isn't that just like a woman," (3) quality of Black models, and (4) inadequacy in dealing with death. This is a good consciousness-raising film for parents because it discusses sensitivity toward children's problems. Evaluate whether or not to use with children. Available in filmstrip with cassette/record and paperback from Baker & Taylor; also available in film from Miller-Brody Productions.

Wilson, Beth P. **The Great Minu.** Follett, 1974. KP

Based on "The Honourable Minu" from West African folktales. Black author teams with Black illustrator and relates tale that deals with materialism and other values. Introduction informs young children about how tales are now told in an African village.

Resources for Adults

Books and Articles

Africa: Man and His Music. Keyboard, January 1973.

Although intended for intermediate and middle school children, this pamphlet contains illustrations from which young children can extract ideas. Art forms are explored—sculpture, leathercraft, and jewelry.

African Resources for School and Libraries. African-American Institute, 1977.

This pamphlet lists organizations, reference works, periodicals, and films about Africa.

American Federation of Arts, ed. **New Black Artists.** American Federation of Arts, 1970.

Describes Black artists and their art.

Baking Powder Biscuits. Ebony Jr! 1 (May 1973): 31-32.

A soul food recipe, just right for a classroom activity.

The Black Child and Family: Special Edition. LINC Child Development Training Center.

Articles and a valuable list of resource materials are included in this booklet.

Brooks, Lester. **Great Civilizations of Ancient Africa.** Four Winds, 1971.

This lengthy book focuses on achievements of Black cultures.

Chapman, Abraham, ed. **New Black Voices: An Anthology of Contemporary Afro-American Literature.** Mentor, 1972.

From the "Foreword" by Ben Ali Lumumba to the "Founding Address" by C. Eric Lincoln, the reader realizes that there is "no aspect of the culture of this nation which has not been touched by the black presence; by what we have said and by what we have done." Critical essays by Eldridge Cleaver, James Baldwin, and Darwin Turner are impressive. A sizable section of poetry includes contemporary sounds of Gwendolyn Brooks, Margaret Walker, John O'Neal, Nayo (Barbara Malcolm), Ed Roberson, and Larry Neal.

Comer, James P., and A. F. Poussaint. **Black Child Care. How to Bring Up a Healthy Black Child in America: A Guide to Emotional and Psychological Development.** Simon and Schuster, 1975.

Until this book, books on child care were written for middle-class White families, with White child behavior assumed to be the norm. The authors, Black psychiatrists, believe that growing up Black in America poses many special problems for Black parents. Their book discusses, in question-and-answer format, important issues and problems facing Black parents.

Black Americans

Courlander, Harold. **A Treasury of African Folklore.** Crown, 1975.

Songs, games, folktales, poetry, and sayings may be shared with young children.

Crane, Louise. **The Land and People of the Congo.** Lippincott, 1971.

Interesting facts about the land, people, and culture of the Congo. Good section on art and music.

Culliman, Bernice, ed. **Black Dialects and Reading.** National Council of Teachers of English, 1974.

Examines the interrelationship among Black dialect, oral language, and reading.

Dillard, J. L. **Black English.** Random House, 1972.

Research about Black English history and usage. Because Black dialects are highly regular, precise, and have rules, Black people are bilingual speakers. This book is especially meaningful in encouraging acceptance and understanding of Black dialects.

Du Bois, W. E. B. **The Souls of Black Folk.** Fawcett, 1961.

A literary classic, these fourteen essays involve the reader in an experience of major importance. The new approach to social reform, nonviolent activism, and personal recollections is moving as are the historical sketches stating the "negro's case against the prevailing white attitudes that relegated him to non-citizen status."

Durham, Philip, and E. L. Jones. **The Negro Cowboys.** Dodd, Mead, 1965.

About Black cowboys in America.

Haley, Alex. **Roots.** Doubleday, 1976.

Through twelve years of searching, Haley traced his family back through slavery to his roots in Gambia, Africa. The book dramatizes seven generations in family history, following the history of Kunta Kinte's descendants through the Civil War years into the present.

Hall, Susan J. **Africa in U.S. Educational Materials.** African-American Institute, 1977.

In-depth examination of stereotypes and misconceptions commonly found in educational materials about Africa. Invaluable for all teachers.

Harrison-Ross, Phyllis, and B. Wyden. **The Black Child.** Wyden, 1973.

A parents' guide for rearing children. Helps Black parents and teachers deal with problems of the young Black child growing up in America, and helps White parents and teachers raise their consciousnesses on how racial prejudice is taught to young children.

How the Monkey Got Its Tail. *Ebony Jr!* 1 (January 1974): 46-50.

A lion who leaps and licks, a pecking peacock who peeps and pecks, in a bold flash of illustrations.

Fanon, Frantz. **Black Skin, White Masks: The Experiences of a Black Man in a White World.** Grove, 1967.

This study relays the message that "truly what is to be done is to set man free," that the Black is no more to be loved than anyone, and "that it be possible for me to discover and to love man, wherever he may be." Fanon's final prayer, "O My Body, make of me always a man who questions!" summons one to explore the writings and art forms of all cultures.

Hughes, Langston. **Selected Poems.** Knopf, 1971.

Hughes's poems foster expressions in dance and painting.

Latimer, Bettye I., ed. **Starting Out Right: Choosing Books about Black People for Young Children.** Wisconsin Department of Public Instruction, 1972.

Provides a conceptual framework for children's books dealing with Black Americans by offering guidelines and rationale for examining literature.

Resources for Adults

Leab, Daniel J. **From Sambo to Superspade.** Houghton Mifflin, 1975.

The development of the Black image in motion pictures is traced in chronological order. In the past, "the movies presented blacks as subhuman, simpleminded, superstitious, and submissive." Today "superspade can do no wrong and almost always comes out on top." Both types of images are caricatures. Because movies and television are so much a part of children's lives, adults must be aware of how Black Americans are portrayed and select portrayals which are authentic. The author hopes that in the future, the Black image will portray "dimensions of humanity" for all Americans.

MacCann, Donnarae, and G. Woodard. **The Black American in Books for Children: Readings in Racism.** Scarecrow, 1972.

Readings give examples of racism in popular and universally read books. Good insight and guidelines for establishing criteria for detection of racism.

McLaughlin, Clara J., and others. **The Black Parents' Handbook: A Guide to Healthy Pregnancy, Birth, and Child Care.** Harcourt Brace Jovanovich, 1976.

The first book of its kind for Black parents. According to the Black authors, developmental patterns and needs of Black children are not the same as those of children from other ethnic groups.

Ojigbo, A. Okion. **What It Means to Be Young and Black in Africa.** Random House, 1971.

Adults can gain new insight from this book about growing up in Africa. This book supports study of the Black culture.

Pugh, Roderick W. **Psychology and the Black Experience.** Brooks/Cole, 1972.

The nature of Black experience and struggle for personal integrity in America are discussed by Black psychologists. Insightful chapters on what it means to be Black.

Rush, Theressa G., and others. **Black American Writers Past and Present: A Biographical and Bibliographical Dictionary.** 2 vols. Scarecrow, 1975.

Furnishes information about the lives and works of more than 2,000 Black American writers from the early eighteenth century to the present.

Schockley, Ann A., and S. P. Chandler, eds. **Living Black American Authors.** Bowker, 1973.

A biographical directory. Source for identifying 425 Black authors who are writing today. Covers artists, educators, business persons, novelists, poets, film critics, publishers, and media specialists.

Sharpe, Maya. **An African Mask Is in Your Kitchen.** *Ebony Jr!* 1 (June/July 1973): 32-33.

"Use your imagination when you make your masks." Recipes, photographs, and notes about how African artists make masks.

Smythe, Mabel M., ed. **The Black American Reference Book.** Prentice-Hall, 1975.

Brings together a comprehensive view of the world of Black Americans: history, personality pressures; social and economic status; involvement in and contribution to arts and letters; participation and treatment in the popular media, sports, and the armed forces; and other related subjects. Valuable source material.

Van Doren, Charles, ed. **The Negro in American History.** Encyclopaedia Britannica, 1972.

Articles by different authors, illustrated with photographs, covering the years 1567-1971. Helpful background information.

Wari, Wari. *Ebony Jr!* 1 (January 1974): 28-29.

Directions for making and playing Wari, the most popular game played in Africa. Also known as Oware, Ayo, Kala, and

Mancala, this game originated in Africa and is presently played everywhere from the southern tip of Africa through Asia to Hawaii.

Bibliographies

Hudson, Ralph, ed. **Black Art.** National Art Education Association, 1970.

A bibliography of Afro-American art; also includes books, monographs, exhibition catalogs, periodicals, and related material.

Mills, Joyce W., ed. **The Black World in Literature for Children: Print and Nonprint Materials.** Atlanta University, School of Library Service, 1975.

"Informative Trend" sections give background and current status of authors and illustrators. Numerous early childhood books and materials may be located in section for older children. Confusing organization but well worth the searching to locate the abundance of nonprint and print materials.

Schmidt, Nancy J. **Selected Bibliographies for Teaching Children about Subsaharan Africa.** ICBD, 1975.

Selected materials for children to learn about Africa. Young children are included in the section "Books for Teaching about Africa, Grades K Through 2." "Debunking Myths about Africa" is especially appropriate for adults. Author's studies in anthropology, focused on Africa, enable her to give a critical review of materials which are current, accurate, and unbiased.

Catalogs

Afro-American Publishing Co.

Distributes posters, records, games, and books including Ella Jenkins records. Materials for adults and for young children. Request catalog of multimedia materials.

School Services Division, African American Institute.

A national program concerned with informing Americans about Africa. A brochure which lists available materials, including descriptions and prices, will be sent on request. Request catalog for teaching/learning materials.

Periodicals

Black Information Index.

Published by a consortium of Black libraries. Focuses on bibliographies, book reviews, and source materials. Attempts to keep readers up-to-date.

Ebony. Johnson Publishing Co.

A pictorial monthly of wide general circulation. Includes Black news and cultural events. Source for pictures of Black Americans.

Ebony Jr! Johnson Publishing Co.

Black magazine with articles, stories, poems, pictures, and creative ideas for children.

The Journal of Negro Education. Howard University.

Of interest to teachers, Black or White. Articles on education, book reviews, and bibliographies of current publications.

The Journal of Negro History. Association for the Study of Negro Life and History.

Covers the field of history and Black culture.

Materials and Experiences

Posters/Pictures

Black ABC's: Picture Story Prints. Society for Visual Education.

Vividly illustrated alphabet posters (26 prints in color) with emphasis on Black culture. Valuable for use with all children.

The Black Experience in Children's Audiovisual. New York Public Library, Office of Children's Services.

Records, cassettes, films, filmstrips, multimedia kits, and directories of sources are included in this thirty-two page booklet. Annotations and descriptive text assist in selecting materials for young children.

Children Around the World. Society for Visual Education.

Six sets of color photos 18" x 13". SP-131. Children of Africa portrays children and people of Masia, school children of Ethiopia, and Kivi of the Desert.

Dandelion Poster. Library Promotionals.

Poster with Black child inspecting a dandelion. 17" x 23".

Jambo Means Hello Posters. Dial/Delacorte, School and Library Services.

Posters and bookmarks available free. Muriel Feelings illustrates poster, as she did in Swahili alphabet book.

Ward, Olivia T., with music by F. and R. Como. **The ABC's of Black History.** Tandem.

Program consisting of teacher's manual, picture-poster cards with famous Black Americans, songbook, and cassettes.

Records

African Noel. *Making Music Your Own.* Six-record album. Produced by Silver Burdett. Distributed by General Learning Corporation. Album #75180.

This Liberian folksong is brief, and young children learn the lyrics easily.

Afro Rhythms, with Montego Joe. Produced by Kimbo Educational Records. Distributed by Educational Activities. Album #6060.

Sixteen African rhythms encourage creative responses and improvisation. Accompanying booklet enables adult to give some direction to dances from Africa, Haiti, Trinidad, Cuba, and Puerto Rico.

Angela, with Angela Denise Simpson. One record. Produced by Spectrum Records. Distributed by Stallman Educational Systems.

Six-year-old poet records her "Black Children's Poetry." Young children, especially Black children, relate to the poems as they are recited by Angela or sung by John Bennings. Ruby Brown contributes "Bellwoods Trinity Park" and "I Just Want to Be." Manual is included.

Best Record Books for Early Childhood. Children's Music Center.

Distributor of African instruments—bongos, hand rhythm drums, and rattles. Also have an African drum record with Ella Jenkins.

Black and White, with Three Dog Night. One record. Produced by Dunhill Records. Distributed by ABC Records.

"The child is black, the child is white, together they learn to read and write." Children learn this tune quickly and respond to the words.

Caldmon Records.

Folktales from Africa and China. Ossie Davis records Verna Aardema's interpretation of *Zulu*. Catalog lists but does not include descriptions of new record releases. Categorized by age.

Ethnic Dances of Black People Around the World, with Marie Brooks. Produced by Kimbo Educational Records. Distributed by Educational Activities. Album #9040.

Music encourages creative and interpretive movement for young children. Adult adapts dance steps from manual for use with young children.

Jambo and Other Call and Response Songs and Chants, with Ella Jenkins. One record. Produced by Folkways Records. Distributed by Scholastic Records. Also available from Lyons.

Ella Jenkins performs twelve of her famous response songs, including counting in Swahili.

Little Johnny Brown, with Ella Jenkins. One record. Produced by Folkways Records. Distributed by Scholastic Records. Record #SC7631.

Collection of songs which have been sung in Black communities for generations. Also included are several civil rights and freedom songs. Some songs which children enjoy singing are: "Little Johnny Brown," "Hammer, Hammer, Hammer," "Miss Mary Mack," "He's Got the Whole World in His Hands," and "Freedom Train."

Lyons.

Distributor of Ella Jenkins's records and books. Request catalog: "Learning Materials for Early Years."

A Ram Sam Sam. *Making Music Your Own.* Six-record album. Produced by Silver Burdett. Distributed by General Learning Corporation. Album #75180.

This folksong from Africa involves children in movement and in singing. Book accompanies album.

Pearl Primus Africa, with Pearl Primus. Three records/cassettes. Produced and distributed by Miller-Brody Productions.

Pleasant, enchanting voice of Pearl Primus, eminent dancer and anthropologist, relates folktales and legends of Africa for young children. Accompanying teacher manual is useful. P601/3 set with record; P6013C set with cassette.

Rhythms of Far Away. *Rhythms of Childhood*, with Ella Jenkins. One record. Produced by Folkways Records. Distributed by Scholastic Records. Record #SC7653.

Freedom and work chants from Africa. "Kum Ba Ya," a spiritual from Liberia in West Africa will be familiar to some and is easily learned by young children. "En Komo Zee Gah Ba Ba" (My Father's Cattle) is a cattle-herding song.

Materials and Experiences

Songs of Sesame Street. Two-record album. Produced by Children's Television Workshop. Distributed by Columbia Records. Record #CS 1069.

Attempts to teach letters, sounds, concepts of "up" and "down," and colors; and explores feelings about friends.

Films/Filmstrips

Dayrell, Elphinstone. **Why the Sun and the Moon Live in the Sky.** Children's Storybook Theatre. Produced and distributed by ACI Films.

Nigerian folktale based on book relates episode between Water and Sun who were friends; African design illustrates folktale creatively. Children applaud this one! Related stories in the set for K-6 are "Janjo: A Portuguese Tale," "The Old Sheepdog," and "The Stolen Necklace." ACI films available on rental basis. Request list of rental libraries. Four filmstrips/cassettes/teacher's guide.

Wild Green Things in the City. Produced and distributed by ACI Films.

A Black girl searches for green things in the city. Absence of narration encourages young children to comment on young girl's involvement with the plants. Children notice that "she is digging the flowers and getting the roots." Ecologically important. Eleven minutes, 16mm color. ACI films available on rental basis. Request list of rental libraries.

Slides

Travel Slides. Produced by Technicolor Corporation. Distributed by Slides Unlimited.

Request a catalog of slides. Dallas area residents may select slides from the files.

Dolls

Shindana Toys.

Black dolls and games with Black and Afro-American context. Order catalog of complete line of Shindana dolls and games.

Museums

Thum, Marcella. **Exploring Black America: A History and Guide.** Atheneum, 1975.

Guide to the museums, monuments, and historic sites that commemorate the achievements of Black Americans; plus discussions about slavery, the underground railroad, abolitionists, pioneers and cowboys, military heroes, artists and craftsworkers, authors and historians, musicians, scholars, and scientists. Reading level: age ten plus.

American Museum of Natural History.

One of the most interesting collections on African culture in the United States. The exhibit areas are built to resemble African round houses—with green carpeting underfoot, the sound of African music, and even the scent of grass and forest air—of 1,000 diverse groups.

Anacostia Neighborhood Museum.

Opened in 1967, this museum is a combination historical museum, cultural arts center, and meeting place for neighborhood groups. Some of its constantly changing exhibits have had the following titles: "The Douglass Years," "This Thing Called Jazz," "Black Patriots of the American Revolution," "This Is Africa," and "Science, Man's Greatest Adventure."

Partly supported by the Smithsonian Institution and private donations, the museum also sponsors traveling historical and art exhibits, as well as film programs and handicraft classes for children of all ages.

Black History Exhibit Center. Under the sponsorship of the Nassau County Museum.

Blacks were among the first settlers of colonial Long Island. This center tells of the accomplishments of these Americans as well as later Black residents. The center features objects, photographs, and works of local Black artists.

Howard University Gallery of Art.

One of the finest collections of contemporary Black art and African art. The African collection was begun by Alain Locke, the author, historian, and philosopher who gave his personal collection to the gallery.

Los Angeles County Museum of Natural History.

A diorama of the first Black and White settlers arriving in Los Angeles, along with other exhibits on the early history of California.

Museum of African Art.

This collection of art forms housed in the Frederick Douglass Institute includes traditional African sculpture, textiles, and musical instruments. The museum shop displays reproductions, books, jewelry, and prints. Tours daily.

Museum of Black History.

Focuses on the contributions of Black people who have lived in Nebraska, Iowa, North Dakota, South Dakota, Missouri, and Colorado since the Emancipation Proclamation. Only museum of its kind west of the Mississippi.

National Collection of Fine Arts.

Features a survey of two centuries of American art and has an extensive collection of paintings and sculptures by Black American artists. The National Portrait Gallery, in the south wing of this museum, contains forty portraits of famous Black Americans.

National Museum of Natural History.

The Africa Hall has a broad collection of exhibits that explain the lifestyle of the traditional African, who still may be found in rural Africa. Artifacts displayed include African art, household implements, dance costumes, musical instruments, and religious items.

The Oakland Museum.

The many Black Americans who contributed to the settlement and growth of California are well represented by exhibits in this museum.

The displays tell the story of Alvin Coffey, a successful gold miner who became the only Black member of the Society of California Pioneers; Colonel Allensworth, who founded a town in California; Grafton T. Brown, Black artist and lithographer; Captain William T. Shorey, the only Black whaling captain of the Pacific Coast; and many others.

Fisk University Library.

An extensive collection of materials on Blacks in Africa, America, and the Caribbean, including books, phonograph records, sheet music, magazines, and newspapers. The MacDonald Collection of African Art and the Alfred Stieglitz Art Collection are on the third floor.

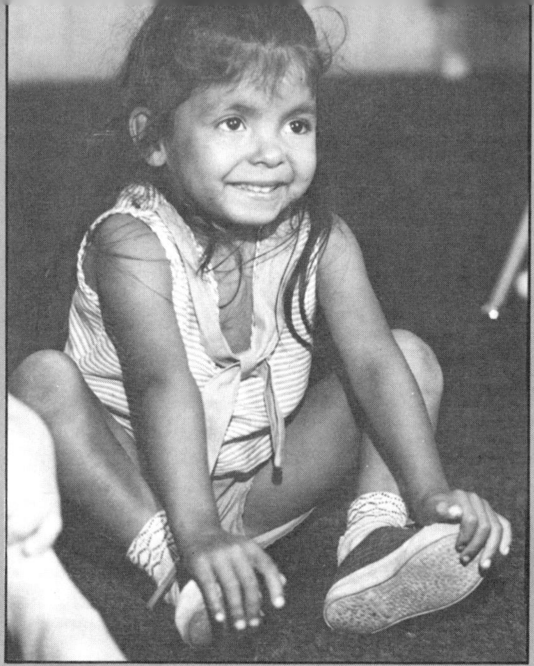

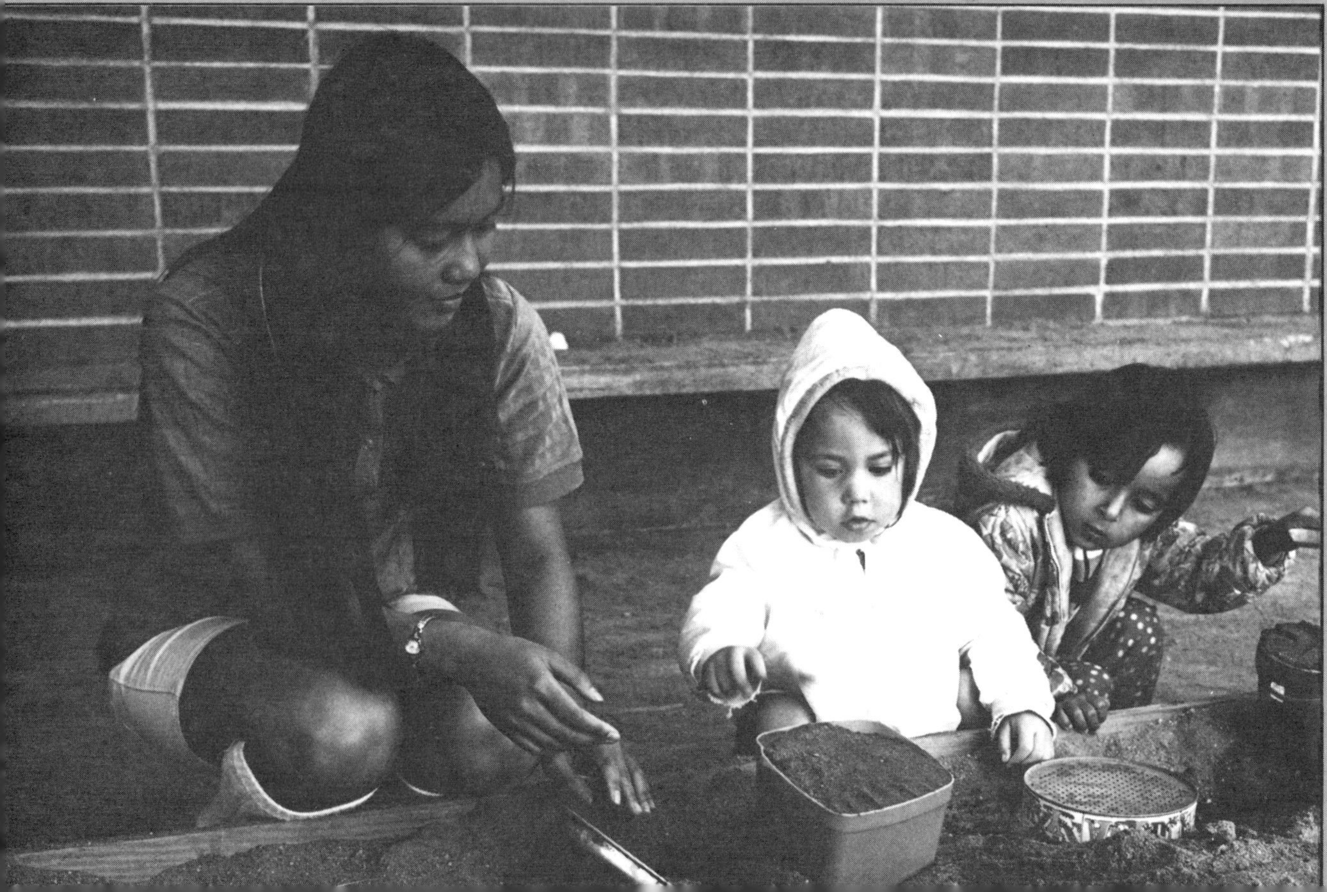

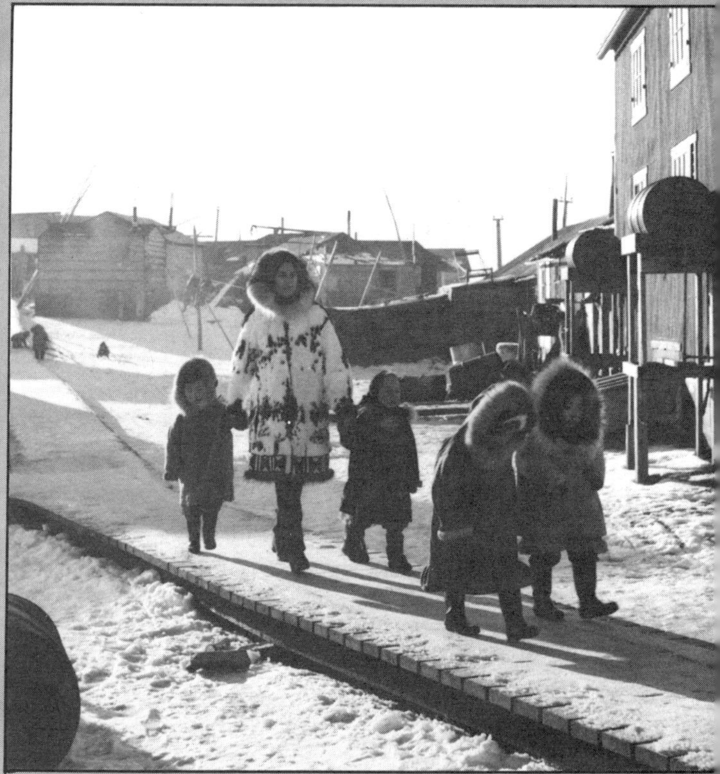

Native Americans

Books for Children

Aliki. **Corn Is Maize: The Gift of the Indians.** Crowell, 1976. KP

   This nonfiction book communicates a number of valuable ideas to children—the relationship between people and nature, interdependence between people, facts about corn. Conveys pride in Native American heritage.

Allen, Terry, ed. **The Whispering Wind: Poetry by Young Indians.** Doubleday, 1972. KP

   Share biography with young children to introduce the poem "Celebration" by Aloza Lopez. Calvin O'John tells of "Dancing Tepees" in the Rocky Mountains.

Bahnimptewa, Cliff. **Dancing Kachinas: A Hopi Artist's Documentary.** The Heard Museum of Anthropology and Primitive Art, Andy Chuka Printers, 1971. KP

   Young children can browse through 285 paintings of Hopi Kachina dances.

Baldwin, Gordon C. **Games of the American Indian.** Norton, 1969. KP

   Games are closely tied to the customs of each Indian nation. Many games are linked to rituals and initiate particular celebrations; however, many are played at other times for amusement and recreation. Instructions for games are included.

Bauer, Helen. **California Indian Days.** Doubleday, 1963. KP

   This history presents Native Americans in California. Photographs add to the authenticity of the book. Text is adaptable for young children.

Baylor, Byrd. **They Put on Masks.** Scribner's, 1975. KP

   A poetic text woven around masks—masks made of beads and string, ivory, turquoise and flowers, "of magic and dreams and the oldest dark secrets of life." Explains the symbolism, rituals, and creation of the many masks important to some Indian people. The book concludes with the tantalizing challenge, "Now think what mask you can make!"

Baylor, Byrd. **When Clay Sings.** Scribner's, 1972. KP

   Text expresses reverence for bits of clay. "They say that every piece of clay is a piece of someone's life." Illustrations by Tom Banti are of black, brown, and cream combination and complement the story written by an Indian author. Children can learn to appreciate pottery as a link in history.

Bealer, Alex W. **The Picture Skin Story.** Holiday House, 1957. KP

   The adventures of Red Bird capture the interest of children. Some children create their own story skin.

Berke, Ernest. **The North American Indians.** Doubleday, 1963. KP

   Display this book when engaging in a study of societies. Children learn about foods, games, and crafts from the detailed text and illustrations.

Native Americans

Bierhorst, John, ed. **The Fire Plume: Legends of the American Indians.** Dial, 1969. KPA

Legends about magicians, adventures, chiefs, and princesses to relate to young children. Adult text is illustrated sparsely with pen and ink drawings.

Bierhorst, John. **The Ring in the Prairie: A Shawnee Legend.** Dial, 1970. KP

White Hawk walks unafraid through the gloomy woods tracing a strange circle. This adventure story was collected by Henry Rowe School Craft and records the authentic remnants of a rapidly vanishing culture. Fascinating color illustrations complete the legend.

Boyd, Enda M. **The Basic Reader.** Navajo Nation, 1975. KP

Primer-first reader in workbook format. Written for young adults who need beginning reading materials. All material is factually correct and has been approved by the Navajos.

Boyd, Edna M. **Navajo Heritage.** Navajo Nation, 1975. KP

Written on a fourth grade reading level, this book deals with the geography of the reservation, the history of the Navajos, and the biographies of famous Navajo leaders and of White friends of the Navajos.

Breetveld, Jim. **Getting to Know Alaska.** Coward, McCann & Geoghegan, 1958. KP

Text is for adults and older children. Illustrations of ivory carvings, kayak lessons, sled riding, and the celebration of "Nullikulltick."

Brewster, Benjamin. **The First Book of Eskimos.** Watts, 1952. KP

The text, which can be read to young children, is a story told from the personal view of a family. Facts are inserted in nonfiction style. Illustrations are descriptive, but life in the fifties was different from lifestyles of some Eskimos today. Use as supplementary resource.

Brewster, Benjamin. **The First Book of Indians.** Watts, 1950. KP

This vividly illustrated book examines the rich heritage of Native Americans. Illustrated are silversmiths, weavers, and Kachina masks.

Brindze, Ruth. **The Story of the Totem Pole.** Vanguard, 1951. KP

Describes how Northwest Coast Indians used poles for their storytelling records. Can be adapted for young children. Provides material which may initiate the creation of totem poles.

Butler, Evelyn, and G. A. Dale. **Alaska: The Land and the People.** Viking, 1957. KP

Glacier beds, totem poles, sled dog puppies, and a porcupine are among good photographs in this book for older children.

Chafetz, Henry. **Thunderbird and Other Stories.** Pantheon, 1964. KP

Nasan, a one hundred foot high giant, who lived with the Indians, becomes the Thunderbird. Adults can tell folktales and display pictures of Indian designs and symbols.

Claiborne, Robert. **The First Americans.** Time-Life, 1973. KP

A book which gives insight into the history and rich cultural background of the Eskimos, Northwest Indians, Southwest Indians, and the Mound Builders. Photographs and drawings are an important facet of the book.

Clark, Ann N. **The Desert People.** Viking, 1962. KP

A boy of the Desert People tells about his village, the roles of his parents, and his philosophy. This book-length poem offers insight into Desert Indian cultures.

Clark, Ann N. **In My Mother's House.** Viking, 1941. KP

Book-length poem gives special insight about Desert Indians.

Books for Children

Clark, Ann N. **The Little Indian Basket Maker.** Melmont, 1957. KP

> Story of Papago girl and her grandmother as they prepare to weave baskets. Directions for weaving are included.

Clymer, Theodore. **Four Corners of the Sky: Poems, Chants and Oratory.** Little, Brown, 1975. KP

> Expressions of hope and despair from numerous Indian cultures in exceptional use of design, symbols, and color with a selection of chants, poems, and songs. Young children appreciate the bold color illustrations by Marc Brown. A high point in literary experience; every classroom and home with concern for North American culture will want to own this book.

Clymer, Theodore. **The Travels of Atunga.** Little, Brown, 1973. KP

> Atunga seeks help from Tungarsug and Sedna, "gods that the Eskimo fears." Language and lifestyle of this Eskimo culture are exemplified in this rare book. Crayon drawings are exquisite.

Cody, Iron Eyes. **Indian Sign Talk in Pictures.** Naturegraph, 1953. KP

> Signs are not identified by specific nation, but young children can learn signs and create new ones as a vehicle for stressing the importance of nonverbal communication.

Copeland, Donalda M. **I Want to Know about Pebbles, Shells, Honeybees and Little Eskimos.** Vol. 2. Children's Press, 1954. KP

> Lifestyle of a Hudson Bay family is introduced through Amak and Toeta.

Creekmore, Raymond. **Lokoshi Learns to Hunt Seals.** Macmillan, 1946. KP

> When ten-year-old Lokoshi goes on a seal hunt, he is permitted to ride on a sled over the rough broken ice, to build an igloo at a sealing camp, and to fish with a harpoon. Adventure gives ideas for activities.

Crompton, Anne E. **The Winter Wife: An Abenaki Folktale.** Little, Brown, 1975. KP

> Themes of a broken promise and of a people who return to wild animal form interest children as does the lifestyle of a hunter. Watercolor paintings in subtle tones express a sensitiveness about relationships.

Crowder, Jack L. **Stefanii dóó MA'll.** Crowder, 1969. KP

> Bilingual text relates adventure of Stefanii, a young Navajo girl, in search of her goat. Designed to enable Navajos to read in their own language.

D'Amato, Janet, and A. D'Amato. **Indian Crafts.** Lion, 1968. KP

> Book of crafts recognizes the skill and creative talents of Native Americans. Pueblo dwelling and ceremonial club and drums are among the handcrafts especially appealing to young children.

Dockstader, Frederick J. **Indian Art of the Americas.** Museum of the American Indian Heye Foundation, 1973. KP

> Brief text with large color and black and white photographs of Indian art from North, Central, and South America.

Dozier, Edward P. **Hano: A Tewa Indian Community in Arizona.** Holt, Rinehart and Winston, 1966. KPA

> Author, who speaks Tewa, gives an intimate, sensitive history of the community. Young children study the full-page black and white photographs.

Erdoes, Richard. **The Sun Dance People.** Knopf, 1972. KPA

> The past and present lives of Plains Indians. Vivid photographs. Adult resource.

Estep, Irene. **Iroquois.** Melmont, 1961. KP

> Longhouses, Green Corn Festival, lacrosse, and Strawberry Festival are unique to the Iroquois. Text can be adapted for young children.

Estep, Irene. **Seminoles.** Melmont, 1963. KP

> Describes activities that distinguish the Seminole. Boxing games, chickee, and headdresses are illustrated.

Feder, Norma. **North American Indian Painting.** Abrams, 1965. KP

> Photographs of museum specimens and a text that focuses on Native American cultural differences in using materials and applying their technique. Text is divided into cultural areas.

Fletcher, Sydney E. **The American Indians.** Grosset and Dunlap, 1972. KP

> Descriptive text and pictures inform young children about implements, equipment, totem poles, canoes, bear hunts, games, and toys.

Floethe, Louise L. **The Indian and His Pueblo.** Scribner's, 1960. KP

> Pueblo living in New Mexico is presented in detailed drawings and interesting text. Appeals to young children but is also a valuable resource for adults.

Ginsburg, Mirra. **The Proud Maiden, Tungak, and the Sun.** Macmillan, 1974. KP

> The Eskimo legend relates an adventure of a woman who flees from Tungak, an evil spirit of the Tundra. Told with the use of illustrations, the story is meaningful to young children.

Glubok, Shirley. **The Art of the Eskimo.** Harper & Row, 1964. KP

> One of Glubok's treats. Essential for planning Eskimo cultural awareness. Excellent photographs of actual art forms, masks, and carvings.

Glubok, Shirley. **The Art of the Southwest Indians.** Macmillan, 1971. KP

> Useful photographs provide ideas about basket-weaving, sandpainting, rock pictures, and Kachina masks. Nations are identified.

Goetz, Delia. **The Arctic Tundra.** Morrow, 1958. KP

> Describes seasons in the Arctic in a way young children can understand. Good section on animals.

Greenlee, Donna. **The Navajo Design Book.** Fun Publishing, 1975. KPA

> Typical designs from sandpainting are recreated in this color book. The book is suggested not as a creative endeavor but for an appreciation of the designs in Indian art forms of weaving, jewelry making, and sandpainting.

Grimm, William C. **Indian Harvests.** McGraw-Hill, 1973. KP

> Chestnuts, crabapples, pinyon nuts, and yampa have been harvested by American Indians as the bounty of the land provided rich feasts. Fosters insight about the heritage of Indian agriculture.

Hall, Geraldine. **Kee's Home: A Beginning Navajo/English Reader.** Northland, 1971. KP

> Renewed interest of the Navajo to learn to read their own language initiated the writing of this book. Large pencil illustrations with a sentence in Navajo and in English depict life in a Navajo village.

Haury, Emil W. **The Hokokam.** *National Geographic* 139 (May 1967): 670-701. National Geographic Society. KPA

> Culture of a courageous people, the Hokokam, is explored through treasures restored by archaeologists. Photographs for young children, with the text for adults.

Heady, Eleanor B. **Sage Smoke: Tales of the Shoshoni-Bannoch Indians.** Follett, 1973. KPA

> The folklorist/author collected tales from Indians at the Fort Hall reservation. Adult text expresses Shoshoni's reverence for nature. Display illustrations by Arvis Stewart while telling the tale to children who recall the adventure stories of Bambooka, Moppo, and Ejupa.

Books for Children

Herbert, Wally. **Polar Deserts.** Watts, 1971. KPA

   Dog teams making their crossings between ice floes, children's faces, mother dressing her child, and Eskimo child feigning a caribou—all are captured in full-page photographs in color. Text for adults.

Hermanns, Ralph. **Children of the North Pole.** Harcourt Brace Jovanovich, 1963. NKP

   Eskimo lifestyle is explored in a text which is appropriate to read to young children. Authentic photographs of Greenlanders enhance appreciation of Eskimo cultures.

Hesse, Zora G. **Southwestern Indian Recipe Book: Apache, Papago, Pima, Pueblo, and Navajo.** Filter, 1973.

   Traditional recipes with modern variations. Recipes for breads, stews, drinks, and vegetables are illustrated with pencil drawings. Purchase from Hopi Silvercraft Cooperative Guild.

Hodges, Margaret. **The Fire Bringer: A Paiute Indian Legend.** Little, Brown, 1972. KP

   A coyote is counselor and a young boy is the leader as they involve Paiutes in an endeavor to bring fire from Burning Mountain. The illustrations by Peter Parnall offer an experience in design, color, and descriptive images.

Hofsinde, Robert (Gray Wolf). **Indian Arts.** Morrow, 1971. KP

   Describes clay, copper, and silver; roots, wood, stone, and shell crafts; food bowls of clay; and weaving with grasses. Ideas for painting symbols on stone.

Hofsinde, Robert (Gray Wolf). **Indian Costumes.** Morrow, 1968. KPA

   Informative text for adults. Drawings of costumes made from museum collection. Distinguishes attire by nation.

Hofsinde, Robert (Gray Wolf). **Indian Games & Crafts.** Morrow, 1967. KP

   Two favorite areas of any culture—games and crafts. Simple diagrams for crafts are included. An excellent resource.

Hofsinde, Robert (Gray Wolf). **Indian Music Makers.** Morrow, 1967. KP

   Directions for making musical instruments. An excellent historical background of each is included.

Hofsinde, Robert (Gray Wolf). **Indian Picture Writing.** Morrow, 1959. KP

   Examines the method used to symbolize thoughts with pictures. Children may copy symbols and create their own stories.

Hofsinde, Robert (Gray Wolf). **Indian Sign Language.** Morrow, 1956. KP

   Includes necessary words, descriptions of how to make the signs, and illustrations showing the sign being made. An excellent resource.

Hofsinde, Robert (Gray Wolf). **The Indians' Secret World.** Morrow, 1955. KP

   Numerous tales for children. Mask, pipe, and moccasins are significant. Illustrations by Gray Wolf are descriptive.

Hopkins, Marjorie. **The Three Visitors.** Parents' Magazine Press, 1967. KP

   An ivory fish carving presented to Nuka Cham by a pelican begins an adventure for the young girl and her aged aunt as they wait in an ice igloo for great-grandmother to return. Young children delight in this tale of decision making. Large colorful illustrations by Anne Rockwell stretch the tale further.

Hughes, Phyllis. **Pueblo Indian Cookbook: Recipes from the Pueblos of the American Southwest.** Museum of New Mexico Press, 1977. KPA

"The world of the Pueblo" is presented in recipes honored and tested by New Mexico Pueblos. Young children delight in making fry bread and frijoles, Pueblo style.

Hunt, Ben W. **Crafts and Hobbies.** Golden, 1962. KP

"Indian Ornaments" section contains complete directions for Indian hair ornaments, rattles, belts, and arm bands which encourage young children to attempt their crafts.

Hunt, Ben W. **Golden Book of Indian Crafts and Lore.** Golden, 1954. KP

Detailed instructions for handcrafts. Splash of Indian lore provides special insight about particular crafts. Helpful section on designs and symbols.

Hunt, Karis, and B. W. Carlson. **Masks and Mask Makers.** Abingdon, 1961. KP

"Eskimo Masks of Alaska" and "Indian Masks" briefly describe a shaman and his many duties. Children can make masks, dance, play tambourines, and call to the spirit in a secret language.

Hyde, Hazel. **Maria Making Pottery.** Sunstone, 1973. KP

A picture-story about a famous San Ildefonso Indian. Vivid photographs relate the complete process of creating a pot from clay. The authenticity of the event as related in this book with brief text is important to young children.

Jacobsen, Daniel. **The Hunters.** Watts, 1974. KPA

Hunting tribes—Comanche, Assiniboin, and Chippewa—are examined in this book for older children and adults. Ink illustrations of a parfleche, bison and caribou hunting scenes, and a Chippewa on snowshoes add to knowledge about the hunting tribes of America.

Jenness, Aylette. **Dwellers of the Tundra: Life in an Alaskan Eskimo Village.** Macmillan, 1970. KPA

Text for adult is excellent and informative. Exceptional and authentic black and white photographs of homes and people.

Jones, Hattie, ed. **Poetry of the North American Indians: The Trees Stand Shining.** Dial, 1971. KP

Songs, prayers, lullabies, and chants in poetic form express Native American view of life, translated from Indian languages. Watercolor paintings complement this beautiful and significant book.

Keating, Bern. **Alaska.** National Geographic Society, 1975. KPA

In beautiful photographs and descriptive text, Alaska is portrayed as America's last great wilderness.

Kirk, Ruth. **David, Young Chief of the Quileutes: An American Indian Today.** Harcourt Brace Jovanovich, 1967. KP

True story of the Quileutes told through the life of its young chief. Explains how Indian life has been changed by the White culture. Superb photographs of beautiful faces and places.

Kobrin, Janet, and M. Bernstein. **How the Sun Made a Promise and Kept It: A Canadian Indian Myth.** Scribner's, 1974. KP

A delightful tale about Weese-ke-jak's mistake in capturing the sun. How Beaver's bravery freed the sun and the promise the sun made in return for his freedom is a beautiful story.

Krenz, Nancy, and P. Byrnes. **Southwestern Arts and Crafts Projects: Ages 5-12.** Sunstone, 1976. KP

Numerous activities of cultural interest for young children. Format enables children to select activity easily.

Books for Children

Lacotawin, Rosebud Yellow Rose. **An Album of American Indian.** Watts, 1969. KP

Photographs of Navajo weaving a rug and illustrations of Indian dances.

La Farge, Olivia. **The American Indian.** Golden, 1960. KP

Based on *A Pictorial History of the American Indian*, this edition is written for young readers. Colorful photographs and illustrations for young children.

La Farge, Olivia. **A Pictorial History of the American Indian.** Crown, 1956. KP

Authentic illustrations in this history make it an excellent resource book when exploring the Native American culture. Ideas for murals, masks, and hunting equipment. Helps children appreciate Native American contributions.

Lewis, Richard. **I Breathe a New Song: Poems of the Eskimo.** Simon and Schuster, 1971. KPA

"Poems are a result of poetic acts by individual Eskimos." As in their carvings, the Eskimo waits until a form reveals itself. Words are freed and "words fade away like hills in a fog." To read these poems is to have a peek inside a culture, where the spirit and soul of the Eskimo are revealed. Excellent book for selecting poems to read to young children. Graphic illustrations are by Oonark, a significant contemporary artist.

Lucero, Faustina H. **Little Indians' ABC.** ODDO, 1974. NKP

This book helps to fill a void in literature. The Indian children depicted in the book are from thirteen nations which are identified. The author lives on an Indian reservation and writes for Indian and Spanish children. The illustrator, Jeanne Pearson, is known for her paintings of the North American big game animals and her illustrations for books on the American Indian. Her bold, vivid illustrations in this book depict Indians engaged in traditional activities.

Machetanz, Sara. **A Puppy Named Gih.** Scribner's, 1957. KP

Lovable Gih proves that the largest and strongest is not always the best. The story of sled puppies in Alaska is a favorite of young children, and prompts dramatization.

Marriott, Alice. **Winter-Telling Stories.** Crowell, 1969. KPA

Synday was "a funny looking man" who made the world like it is. From these ten winter tales, select stories to tell children. Some children may want to retell and dramatize the stories.

Martin, Fran. **Nine Tales of Coyote.** Harper & Row, 1950. KPA

Folklore of the Nez Perce Indian is presented in a text for adults. Full-page dramatic drawings can be viewed by children as an adult tells the tale. One of few books with Nez Perce tales.

Martin, Patricia M. **Eskimos: People of Alaska.** Parents' Magazine Press, 1970. KP

An informative book, especially the section "Hunting for Seal and Walrus." Illustrations by Robert Frankenburg, using subtle colors, are of interest to children.

Martin, Patricia M. **Indians: The First Americans.** Parents' Magazine Press, 1970. KP

Gives general characteristics of nations in four major geographic areas. Last chapter, "What Indians Have Given Us," is meaningful to children as they explore the culture of the "first Americans."

Martin, Patricia M. **Navajo Pet.** Putnam's, 1971. KP

Learning that living on a Navajo reservation means living in a hogan, eating cornmeal mush, riding a horse, and feeding sheep is a special experience for young children.

May, Julian. **Before the Indians.** Holiday House, 1969. KP

This theoretical text is helpful when children pose questions about life before the Indians. Fantastic portrayal of Paleo-Indian by illustrator Symeon Shimin.

Mayberry, Genevieve. **Eskimo of the Little Diomede.** Follett, 1961. KP

Teacher in Alaskan school relates the lifestyle of Eskimos in this community which has embraced many White inventions. Children identify with the Eskimo children who have radios, clocks, outboard motors, and are fascinated by these same Eskimos as they search for eggs and seals and wear heavy furs. Few books portray modern Eskimos as they really live.

McGaw, Jessie B. **Painted Pony Runs Away, As Little Elk Tells It in Indian Picture Writing.** Nelson, 1958. KP

Picture writing is interesting to children for copying, reading, or creating their own symbols. Shows similarities in hieroglyphics of the Chinese, Egyptians, and Native Americans.

McNeer, May. **The Story of the Southwest.** Harper & Row, 1948. KP

Discusses the cliff-dwellers and their culture, includes colorful, detailed drawings of the land of the Pueblos. Children learn that modern Americans were not the first "apartment" dwellers.

Metayer, Maurice, ed. **Tales from the Igloo.** St. Martin's, 1972. KPA

The Eskimo relied mostly on verbal communication to pass on their history, culture, and traditions. Some of the stories are suitable for young children. Foreword and preface contain updated material about changes in contemporary Eskimo culture.

Moon, Grace, and C. Moon. **One Little Indian.** Whitman, 1957. KP

Tells of a happy day in the life of Ah-di, who lives in the desert. Large illustrations of the adventures of this four-year-old boy appeal to some children.

Morrow, Suzanne S. **Inatuk's Friend.** Little, Brown, 1968. NKP

The story explores Eskimo culture. Children learn games and names of Alaskan surroundings. Main value of this story may be the interpersonal relationships.

Newell, Edythe W. **The Rescue of the Sun.** Whitman, 1970. KP

Cultural background material in the introduction acquaints readers with the environment of some Eskimo cultures and conditions surrounding the folktales.

Niethamer, Carolyn. **American Indian Food and Lore: 150 Authentic Recipes.** Macmillan, 1974. KPA

"Arise and make use of the day." Indian women went into the fields as an "ingenious team of lay botanists" to wring the most out of a bleak appearing environment. Introduction and brief sketch give adults interesting facts about harvesters. Young children can prepare sunflower bread and other foods.

Palmer, William R. **Why the North Star Stands Still.** Prentice-Hall, 1957. KA

The Paiute tale explains why they "dance the snake dance," "why the North Star stands still," and "why tobats made winter." Select from twenty-eight tales that capture tradition and culture.

Payne, Elizabeth. **Meet the Native American Indians.** Random House, 1965. KP

Presents many facets of Native American culture and illustrates detailed activities.

Books for Children

Perrine, Mary. **Salt Boy.** Houghton Mifflin, 1968. NKP

    Delightful story about Indian boy's desire to learn to rope "the black horse." Illustrations capture the sensitivity of the boy for animals.

Pine, Tillie S. **The Eskimos Knew.** McGraw-Hill, 1962. NK

    Engages children in scientific experiments and craft experiences. Children can begin to see the Eskimos as conservationists. Illustrations by Ezra Jack Keats.

Pine, Tillie, and J. Levine. **The Incas Knew.** McGraw-Hill, 1968. KP

    Wonders of yesterday and today highlighted in a science activity book about the way the Incas solved problems and the way we use the same principles today. Excellent selection of color, design, and illustrations.

Rachlis, Eugene. **Indians of the Plains.** American Heritage, 1960. KP

    Text and illustrations describe sports and pastimes, arts, sign language, and cattle.

Raskin, Joseph, and E. Raskin. **Indian Tales.** Random House, 1969. KPA

    Adult text can be told to young children in folktale style. Woodcuts are appealing.

Rasmussen, Knud. **Beyond the High Hills: A Book of Eskimo Poems.** World, 1961. NKPA

    Photographs by Guy Mary-Rousseliere qualify the book as an exceptional resource in exploring Eskimo culture. Photos depict the Iglulik as they build a snowhouse, harpoon a bear, and clean a seal. Large photographs of faces, animals, and various styles of homes and clothing are included. Songs recorded in poetic form add to the experience as will the lifestyles depicted here.

Rasmussen, Knud, col. **Eskimo Songs and Stories.** Delacorte, 1975. KP

    "Songs are thoughts, sung out with the breath when people are moved by great forces and ordinary speech no longer suffices." A collection of Netsilik literature and original print selections. Discloses the soul of the rugged life of "the people of the seal." Illustrations by Keakshuk and Publo.

Reynolds, Charles R., Jr. **American Indian Portraits.** Greene, 1971. KP

    Large full-page black and white photographs of Indians of all ages taken in 1913 by the Wanamaker expedition when the sense of national guilt about what had been done to Native Americans was rising.

Rockwell, Anne. **The Dancing Stars: An Iroquois Legend.** Crowell, 1971. KP

    An artist who spent several years as a child on an Indian reservation interprets a popular folktale about two brothers' love for one another.

Roessel, Robert A., Jr., and D. Platero. **Coyote Stories of the Navajo People.** Navajo Curriculum Center Press, 1974. KP

    Aimed at increasing understanding among all people, these folktales enable Navajo children to learn about themselves, and explore the thinking of the culture. *Coyote Stories of the Navajo People* is one in a series being developed at Rough Rock Demonstration School, a school designed for Native American children, to help children develop a positive self-image. The stories are related to various ceremonies and are often told in the hogan by someone from the older generation.

Scheer, George, ed. **Cherokee Animal Tales.** Holiday House, 1968. KP

    Authentic collection of stories about tribal history. Young children delight in listening to stories about animals.

Scherer, Joanna C. **Indians.** Ridge Press Book, Crown, 1973. KP

> The great photographs reveal Native North American life, 1847-1929, from the unique collection of the Smithsonian Institution.

Scott, Ann H. **On Mother's Lap.** McGraw-Hill, 1972. NKP

> Mother's lap is special and can accommodate everyone. This story is a heartwarming, insightful lesson in sharing, related in brief text and soft tones, with illustrations by Glo Coalson. Clothing and home furnishings afford the reader a realistic view of life in one Alaska community. Scott deals with feelings familiar to all young children.

Showers, Paul. **Indian Festivals.** Crowell, 1969. KP

> Describes dances of different nations which can be adapted for young children.

Sleator, William. **The Angry Moon.** Little, Brown, 1970. NKP

> Adapted from a legend of the Tlingit in Alaska, this artist's first book is a favorite with young dramatists.

Southwest Indian Country: Arizona, New Mexico, Southern Utah and Colorado. Lane, 1970. KP

> Features picture writing, tribal festivals, bread making, and the art of Pueblo pottery. Includes ideas for activities.

Stull, Edith. **The First Book of Alaska.** Watts, 1965. KP

> Photographs of brown bear, walrus, and two-foot high cabbage.

Talaswaima, Terrance. **The Birds of Hano Village: A Hopi Indian Story.** Hopi Publishers, Hopi Action Program, 1975. NK

> The curator of the Hopi Museum at Second Mesa, Arizona, translated this Hopi folktale. This region of rocky mesas and sandy valleys is illustrated by Talaswaima with Indian design, earth tones, and black and white drawings. The ever present need for water is the motivating force in the religious rites of the Hopi. The book also includes discussion about language differences within Hopi cultures. The author illustrates himself as a young child in several of the illustrations and young children try to locate him.

Talaswaima, Terrance. **The Eagle Hunt.** Hopi Publishers, Hopi Action Program, 1974. NK

> An eagle hunt engages two Hopi boys. The home dance requires the use of eagles as a sacrifice. The feathers used for prayer bring rain, a constant concern of the desert dwellers.

Talaswaima, Terrance. **Hopi Bride at the Home Dance: A Hopi Indian Story.** Hopi Publishers, Hopi Action Program, 1974. NK

> Account of a wedding ceremony involves young children with a glimpse of the Hopi culture—preparing blue cornmeal batter for piki and wheat pudding (pik'ami), weaving ceremonial wedding robes, and viewing the Kachinas as they dance and present gifts to the people.

Talaswaima, Terrance. **Winter Rabbit Hunts.** Hopi Publishers, Hopi Action Program, 1974. NK

> Told in the first person, this is an account of a rabbit hunt with men and boys from a Hopi village. Another story translated as an educational project of the Hopi Follow Through Program.

Thorneycroft, Edward. **Thunderbird: An Indian Legend.** Rand-McNally, 1972. KP

> Story about nomadic Indians as they seek to be recognized and search for the Thunderbird.

Tomkins, Stuart R. **Life in America: Alaska.** Fideler, 1963. KPA

> Text for adults and older children but photographs are enjoyed by all ages. Young children like the authentic pictures of Eskimo homes, walruses, and fishing through holes in the ice. Helpful ideas for classroom activities.

Books for Children

Tomkins, William. **Indian Sign Language.** Dover, 1969. KP

Dictionary of Indian sign language with illustrations and text.

Toye, William. **The Mountain Goats of Temlaham.** Walck, 1969. KP

Legend of the Micmac of eastern Canada lends itself to drama. Canadian Elizabeth Cleaver illustrates the tale in bold, glowing colors.

Vevers, Gwynne. **Animals of the Arctic.** McGraw-Hill, 1965. KP

A simple science book that introduces the animals that live in the North, and gives facts that interest children. Drawings by Maurice Wilson are in subtle colors.

Warren, Betsy. **Indians: Who Lived in Texas.** Steck-Vaughn, 1970. KP

Insight about history of Texas Indians. Illustrations for ideas about things to create.

Williams, Barbara. **Let's Go to an Indian Cliff Dwelling.** Putnam's, 1965. KP

This book takes children on a trip around Mesa Verde.

Wolf, Bernard. **Tinker and the Medicine Men: The Story of a Navajo Boy of Monument Valley.** Random House, 1973. NKP

A week with Tinker Yazzie in his ancestral home is spent in shearing sheep, weaving rugs, sitting on the sand floor of the hogan eating fried bread made by grandmother, sandpainting, and learning the Peyote Way. The traditional Navajo religious customs are observed by the Yazzie family. Black and white photographs portray authentic experience of a Navajo community. The book places emphasis on preservation of lifestyle of Navajo Nation and enables children to recognize the values of the Navajo.

Wormington, H. M. **The Story of Pueblo Pottery.** Denver Museum of Natural History, 1974. KP

Photographs by A. Neil from the University of Colorado Museum collection include unfired basketmaker bowl, tubular clay pipes, and figurines.

Resources for Adults

Books and Articles

Abernethy, Francis E., ed. **Observations and Reflections on Texas Folklore.** Encino, 1972.

>Articles collected by Texas Folklore Society view people as remaining essentially the same and responding in ways similar to the cavedwellers. Folklore is a demonstration of this kinship. Locate the folklore society in your state.

Albaum, Charlet. **Ojo de Dios: Eye of God.** Grosset and Dunlap, 1972.

>This handcraft was borrowed from an ancient tradition of Pueblo and Mexican Indians. Includes details for weaving various colored yarns for Eye of God. Many shapes and designs can be mastered by young children.

Allen, Terry D., ed. **Arrows Four.** Washington Square, 1974.

>The last of four books of winning prose and poetry by young American Indians who have grown up close to animals and nature and in the harsh realities of childhood experiences. Young children will understand and enjoy some of these selections.

Alternate Thanksgiving Resource Packet. Alternatives.

>Includes a Native American view of this traditional holiday and lists of resources dealing with Native Americans and world hunger.

American Indians: Answers to 101 Questions. U.S. Government Printing Office, Superintendent of Documents.

>Recommended by Hopi Indian resource person as a "cleverly written book that deals with prejudice."

Bahti, Tom. **Southwestern Indian Ceremonies.** K. C. Publications, 1974.

>Contains legends, myths, large photographs, illustrations, and descriptive passages that explain the cultures of Southwest Indian groups. Legends/myths can be told to young children. Colorful descriptive photographs of Kosharez, masks, fetishes, tablita, feathers, and figurines parade across the major part of this book.

Bealer, Alex W. **Only the Names Remain: The Cherokees and the Trail of Tears.** Little, Brown, 1972.

>The White people wanted the Cherokees moved far to the west so that they could farm the fertile valleys of the Cherokee Nation. Text is for older children. Important resource for adults who plan cultural awareness activities for young children. Author of *Picture Skin Story* enlightens readers in this more recent book about the exile of the Native Americans from their homes in the Appalachian Mountains region of Georgia.

Berrill, Jacquelyn. **Wonders of the Arctic.** Dodd, Mead, 1959.

>Animal and bird resource. Interesting facts about wildlife in the Arctic.

Resources for Adults

Bjorkland, Lorence F. **The Bison: The Great American Buffalo.** World, 1970.

    Illustrations with carefully researched information about the bison.

Bleeker, Sonia. **The Eskimo: Arctic Hunters and Trappers.** Morrow, 1966.

    Sections on customs and hunting assist readers in understanding the traditional Eskimo. Provides insight into today's problem—scarcity of game.

Bleeker, Sonia. **Indians of the Longhouse: The Story of the Iroquois.** Morrow, 1950.

    Excellent resource. Northeastern nation's traditional lifestyles are explored.

Boas, Frank, and J. W. Powell. **Introduction to Handbook of American Indian Languages and Indian Linguistic Families of America North of Mexico.** University of Nebraska Press, 1966.

    Source for adults involved in bilingual programs.

Brown, Dee. **Bury My Heart at Wounded Knee.** Holt, Rinehart and Winston, 1970.

    A history of the settling of the Western United States as told by the Native Americans who lost their land and their identity to a doctrine called Manifest Destiny.

Ceram, C. W. **The First American: A Story of North American Archaeology.** Harcourt Brace Jovanovich, 1971.

    Story of prehistoric Indian cultures in North America. Numerous illustrations add to the information in this book.

Costo, Rupert, ed. **Textbooks and the American Indian.** American Indian Historical Society, Indian Historian Press, 1970.

    This annotated bibliography of textbooks on the American Indian critically analyzes the many ways Indians have been depicted falsely. Includes eleven criteria for selecting authentic books. Important information to help young children get a true picture of the Native American.

Courlander, Harold. **People of the Short Blue Corn: Tales and Legends of the Hopi Indians.** Harcourt Brace Jovanovich, 1970.

    History of the seven-hundred-year-old Hopi groups is related through legend. Some of the tales are about supernatural events and offer mystical and magical explanations. "How the People Come from the Lower World" is an excellent tale to tell children. Hopi folklorists suggest substituting your own village name in place of the one used in the tale. Courlander gathered these tales while living with the Hopis, and he retells them just as the Hopis told the tales to him.

Dallas Intertribal Center.

    The director visits schools and shares ideas and materials with young children. Check for a similar center in your community.

Deloria, Vine, Jr. **Custer Died for Your Sins.** Macmillan, 1969.

    A book about the Native American's situation in America as a result of the myths and stereotypes that have been created by White society.

Dutton, Bertha P. **Indians of the American Southwest.** Prentice-Hall, 1975.

    Emphasizing philosophy, drama, poetry, and songs, the book aids in the appreciation of the first Americans and their reactions to their surroundings.

Erdoes, Richard. **The Sun Dance People: The Plains Indians, Their Past and Present.** Knopf, 1972.

    Informative text that seeks to correct some myths about Plains Indians. Contains a glimpse of the past but focuses on modern people on reservations who live in tarpaper shacks and must farm barren land. Photographs and illustrations explore their predicament and provide a visual record of the past.

Forrest, Earle L. **The Snake Dance of the Hopi Indians.** Westernlore, 1961.

   Esoteric nature of this dance generates interest. The colorful dance goes back to the roots of the Hopi.

Gridley, Marion E. **Contemporary American Indian Leaders.** Dodd, Mead, 1972.

   Biographies of twenty-six Native American leaders of today.

Gridley, Marion E. **Indian Tribes of America.** Rand-McNally, 1973.

   Specific information about principal groups, how and where they lived and migrated. Share the illustrations with young children.

Heuman, William. **Famous American Indians.** Dodd, Mead, 1972.

   The lives of nine of the best-known Indians of the North American continent: King Phillip, Pontiac, Joseph Brant, Osceola, Tecumseh, Sequoyah, Chief Joseph, Crazy Horse, and Sitting Bull.

Icolari, Dan. **Reference Encyclopedia of the American Indian. Vol. 2.** 2nd ed. Todd, 1974.

   A listing of American Indians prominent in Indian affairs, business, the arts, and professions.

Indian Education Resources Center.

   Research papers, reports, curriculum bulletins listed.

Judge, Joseph. **Alaska: Rising Northern Star.** *National Geographic* 147 (June 1975): 731-791. National Geographic Society.

   Article describes event at Shishmaref when ship makes its annual port of call.

A Kindergarten Curriculum Guide for Indian Children: A Bilingual-Bicultural Approach. U.S. Department of the Interior, Bureau of Indian Affairs, Indian Education Resources Center.

   Songs, activities, field trips, and bibliography, illustrated by numerous photos of Indian children.

Klein, Barry T. **Reference Encyclopedia of the American Indian. Vol. 1.** 2nd ed. Todd, 1973.

   The most complete compilation of related source materials on the North American Indian ever assembled. Includes government agencies, museums, libraries, associations, monuments and parks, tribal councils, urban Indian centers, schools, college courses, arts and crafts shops, visual aids, government publications and periodicals.

Laxalt, Robert. **New Mexico: The Golden Lands.** *National Geographic* 138 (September 1970): 299-343. National Geographic Society.

   New Mexico remains the home of 77,000 Indians. What it is like to live in New Mexico and how the Indians strive to retain their cultural heritage are explored in this article.

A Letter to White People: The New White Person. *Akwesasne Notes* 1 (Spring 1976): 37. Mohawk Nation.

   Essays comment on White racism. New requirements, new position for developing an "aware" White community are stated. It is imperative that each adult be exposed to messages of this depth.

Looney, Ralph. **The Navajos.** *National Geographic* 142 (December 1972): 741-781. National Geographic Society.

   After the invasion by Whites and a history of broken treaties, neglect, and exploration, modern Navajos are still coping with prejudice and unemployment. Their traditional reverence for land yields to economic pressures.

Resources for Adults

Mary-Rousseliere, Guy. **I Live with the Eskimos.** *National Geographic* 139 (February 1971): 188-217. National Geographic Society.

   On the shivering edge of civilization live the Canadian Eskimos. The article includes photographs of narwhal hunters, landscapes, and families.

McLuhan, Terry C., comp. **Touch the Earth.** Promontory, 1971.

   Passages written by Native Americans. Emphasis on the importance of harmony between people and nature. Illustrated in brown tones.

Mills, Martha D., ed. **Hopi Awareness for the Classroom.** Hopi Tribe.

   Games, recipes, songs, stories, signs, vocabulary, and an introduction to develop understanding of the Hopi culture. This booklet was prepared for a 1976 workshop at Second Mesa and involved several Pueblo groups. Request the booklet sponsored by the U.S. Office of Education.

Popp, James A. **An Examination of Children's Books on the American Indian.** *BIA Education Research Bulletin* 3, no. 1 (1975): 10-23. Bureau of Indian Affairs.

   Reviews forty-nine books for authenticity, depth, usefulness, and stereotyping. Many books are found to be derogatory either in language or illustrations.

Qoyawayma, Polingaysi (Elizabeth Q. White). **No Turning Back: A Hopi Indian's Struggle to Live in Two Worlds.** University of New Mexico Press, 1964.

   A Hopi woman struggles to endure poverty and her own sense of inadequacy outside her native environment. "A true account of a Hopi woman's struggle to bridge the gap between the world of her people and the world of the white man."

Roch, Ernst, ed. **Arts of the Eskimo: Prints.** Barre, 1975.

   Inuit graphic art in the form of original prints serves as a visual record of the history and traditions of the Inuit as well as an esthetic experience.

Rothe, Aline. **Kalitas' People: A History of the Alabama-Coushatta Indians of Texas.** Texian, 1963.

   Resource for adults interested in the last distinct nation in Texas.

Silverberg, Robert. **The Old Ones: Indians of the American Southwest.** New York Graphic Society, 1965.

   The Indians of the pueblos have endured the contamination of the White people but have retained many of their ancient ways.

Simmons, Leo W., ed. **Sun Chief: The Autobiography of a Hopi Indian.** Yale University Press, 1942.

   The Hopi in Oraibi is presented through exploration of the Hopi lifestyle, social organization, and physical environment as experienced by Don C. Talayesva. "A comprehensive case history, reported in the first person, for those who are interested in the development of personality in relation to society and culture."

A Thanksgiving Curriculum: Offering a Native American Viewpoint. People Against Racism in Education.

   Suggestions for classroom activities designed to heighten awareness about Native Americans.

Thomas, Marjorie, comp. **Indian Cultural Units for the Classroom.** Indian Cultural Curriculum Center, 1975.

   Elementary teachers in Tuba City public schools collaborated to produce a manual of over two hundred pages, replete with ideas for activities, games, songs, clothing, and transportation, organized according to tribal group. Excellent resource, includes bibliography.

Thompson, Stith. **The Folktale.** Holt, Rinehart, and Winston, 1946.

>Introduces the reader to most of the great folktales of the world, including Native American folktales.

Thompson, Stith. **Tales of the North American Indians.** Indiana University Press, 1966.

>Shows similarities and differences in the tales from various areas. Read or tell the folktales.

Tite, Mischa. **The Hopi Indians of Old Oraibi: Change and Continuity.** University of Michigan Press, 1972.

>Anthropologist records observations about kinship customs, witchcraft beliefs, medicine men practices, and the purpose of the Kachina. In diary form, Tite reveals his respect for the Hopi people.

Tunis, Edwin. **Indians.** World, 1959.

>Information about nations; characteristics and activities of each.

Underhill, Ruth M. **The Navajos.** University of Oklahoma Press, 1956.

>History of the largest Indian nation in the United States today. From a small beginning in the Southwest, these Earth People are expert weavers, silversmiths, and shepherds.

Underhill, Ruth M. **Red Man's America: A History of Indians in the United States.** University of Chicago Press, 1953.

>Relates significant contributions of various Indian tribes to American life.

Waters, Frank. **Book of the Hopi: The First Revelation of the Hopi's Historical and Religious World View of Life.** Ballantine, 1963.

>An expression by the Hopi of the traditional viewpoint. Myths, legends, mystery plays, and history are explored. Read *Pumpkin Seed Point* to gain an appreciation of the difficulty the author incurred in recording this history. Thirty elders of the Hopi tribes in Oraibi released information so that Hopi culture could be recorded and preserved. "A presentation of a life pattern rooted in the soil of this continent, whose growth is shaped by the same forces that stamp their indigenous seal upon its greatest mountain and smallest insect and whose flowering is yet to come."

Waters, Frank. **Pumpkin Seed Point: Being Within the Hopi.** Swallow, 1969.

>Collaborating with White Bear on *Book of the Hopi*, Waters dealt with hardships at Pumpkin Seed Point. This is the story of the enforced intimacy between Waters and the Bear couple, the fragmentation of relating to two cultures, and the often hopeless task of securing esoteric material from the Hopis of Arizona.

Wright, Barton, and E. Roat. **This Is a Hopi Kachina.** Museum of Northern Arizona, 1973.

>Unique among the Pueblo Indians is the making of Kachina dolls. Colorful photographs and information about these carved figures are intriguing to young children. Hopi religion should not be taught in a classroom with Hopi children without parents' consent, since the Hopi believe that the Kachinas, the spiritual beings, and any aspects of religious ceremonies should never be topics of classroom discussion without consulting the families.

Zuni People. **The Zunis: Self Portrayals.** University of New Mexico Press, 1972.

>The Zunis, in cooperation with the University of Utah Oral History Project, selected forty-six stories of myth, prophecy, and history that best perpetuate their cultural traditions. These stories about battles, creation, and dances can be told to children.

Resources for Adults

Bibliographies

American Indian: An Annotated Bibliography of Selected Library Resources. Institute for Minnesota Indians, WISC Library Services, 1973.

Resources for adults and children.

American Indian Education: An Abstract Bibliography. ICBD Publications Office, 1975.

Documents selected from ERIC microfiche collection pertaining to American Indians. References from many sources. Up-to-date, pertinent, and timesaving tool.

Indian Bibliography. Instructional Service Center, Professional Library.

Request bibliography. Books may be borrowed from a collection written by American Indian authors.

Catalogs

The American Indian Historical Society.

The major objectives of the organization are to preserve and to promote American Indian culture and to advance the education and general welfare of American Indians while preserving their language, philosophy, and values. Publications: *The Indian Historian* (quarterly); *The WeeWish Tree* (bimonthly); *Annual Index to Literature on the American Indian*. Also publishes textbooks.

Bureau of American Ethnology.

Materials are available at a nominal cost.

Bureau of Indian Affairs (BIA).

The twelve area offices of the Bureau of Indian Affairs are resources for materials published by BIA agencies in their areas.

El Dorado Distributors.

Adult references, "mini-libros," and children's books. Request list of available books.

National Indian Education Association.

Promotes relevant education for American Indians.

Navajo Curriculum Center.

Request publication list of books written by the Navajos at the Navajo Curriculum Center at Rough Rock Demonstration School, Arizona. Frequently selections are out of print until funds become available again for reprint. Select from these inexpensive, authentic materials.

Navajo Reading Study.

This series of books is designed to meet needs of Navajo children. Non-Navajo children also benefit from the stories which are cleverly illustrated and designed. Numerous books for young children. Request list of available materials. Nominal fee that covers cost of printing/postage only.

Publications Service. Haskell Institute.

Price list of publications from Bureau of Indian Affairs. Lists books written by persons who have lived with or worked with Indians. Many of the books listed are unavailable—some are temporarily out of print, and others will not be reprinted.

Rough Rock School Board, Inc.

Source for materials representing Indian history from the Indian point of view. Navajo Curriculum Center Press distributes material for Demonstration School.

The United Tribes of North Dakota Development Corporation. American Indian Curriculum Development Program.

Request list of available materials for young children.

Villagra Book Shop.

Generous selection and stock of books about Indian groups. Helpful and knowledgeable personnel assist in selecting appropriate materials.

Periodicals

Alaska: Life on the Last Frontier. Alaska Northwest Publishing.

Magazine usually has feature stories about animals in Alaska, outdoor living, and interesting places to visit. Magazine seeks to revive culture of Alaska and is ecologically oriented.

American Indian: Man and His Music. Keyboard.

Man and His Music is written for older children; however, younger children enjoy hearing the stories, dancing the ceremonial dances, and creating Indian handicrafts described and illustrated in the magazine. Filmstrips, records, and teachers' guides are included.

ERIC/CRESS Newsletter. ERIC Clearinghouse on Rural Education and Small Schools.

Acquires, indexes, abstracts, and disseminates information related to all aspects of American Indian education, Mexican-American education, outdoor education, rural education, and small schools.

Frontier Times. Western Publications.

Magazine has accounts of Western history dealing with events, places, personalities, legends, etc., some of which relate to the Indian and notable Indian historical figures. Many illustrations and photographs.

Hopi Head Start. Hopi Reservation, Follow Through, Home School Newsletter.

Monthly newsletter informs the reader about activities at the Hopi Reservation. Request that your name be placed on the mailing list.

Indian America.

Magazine features current news, poetry, movies, records, crafts, and reviews.

Indian Cultural/Curriculum Center.

This resource center facilitates cultural awareness for the Tuba City public schools, K-8. Artisans—weavers, basketmakers, carvers, potterymakers, and silversmiths—demonstrate their skills. Hopi and Navajo children use the center as a classroom and as an awareness center. Pottery, woven items, clothing, and jewelry are displayed. Books, records, and materials may be checked out by teachers. Write to the center requesting *Awareness*, the newsletter.

Indian Historian. American Indian Historical Society.

This periodical seeks to promote the culture of the American Indian. Excellent resource for exploration of Native American cultures.

International Native Arts and Crafts. Import Publishers.

Features crafts of Native Americans. Articles explore the art of artisans who are utilizing new materials/new equipment and who have not forsaken their heritage. Children are interested in the bright colored photographs of moccasins, leggings, fans, rosettes, pouches, and sandpaintings. An important magazine for the exploration of Native American cultures.

Resources for Adults

Native Americans: Idea Exchange. LINC Leadership Development Program.

A wealth of materials—reading lists, activities for cooking, sandpainting, handcrafts, poems, and book reviews.

New Mexico Magazine.

Photographs, essays, and historical sketches fill the pages of this Native American oriented periodical. Young children browse through the colorful photographs.

Tosan—American Indian People's Inter-Tribal News. Chief Hawk at Setting Sun—United Remnant Band.

Publication informs the Native American community of news, native advertisements and announcements; instruction in native religion, customs, and beliefs; arts and crafts; history; education; etc.

WeeWish Tree. American Indian Historical Society.

Magazine of Native America for young people. Poems by natives about their cultures and games, pictures of Indians in authentic dress, and art enrichment articles.

Materials and Experiences

Posters/Pictures

Akwesasne Notes. Mohawk Nation.

Akwesasne Notes Calendar—17" x 22" drawings of Native American nations with historical information for adults. Akwesasne Notes also distributes posters suitable for use with young children. Posters are: "Three Sisters," "The North American Indian," "The Rush Gatherer—Arikora." Authentic culture is portrayed in a nonstereotyped image.

American Indian Curriculum Development Program.

Program was established with the main objective of developing Plains Indian social studies curricula relevant to the education of Indians and non-Indians. The content promotes respect for minority groups through Indian cultural awareness. Nonprint materials about Indian families, foods, homes, animals, and communities are available for nominal fees. Expensive kits are also available.

American Indians—Yesterday and Today. Cook, 1973.

Twenty-four colorfully illustrated posters (12½" x 17") of Native American cultures. Manual is by Native American scholars and educators. Poster #61622; manual #65029.

Coyote and Deer. Curriculum Center.

One of the numerous booklet/cassette selections from the Curriculum Center. Available in Navajo and English. Prompt service. Young children delight in "reading" booklet while listening to tape. Real nature sounds are inserted.

Grey Mare. Curriculum Center.

Cassette/booklet. Children delight in hearing folktale about the grey mare. Available in Navajo and English. Order list of other materials available from the center.

Indians of the United States and Canada: Picture Story Study Prints —1300. Society for Visual Education.

Prints are divided into major cultural groups: Northeast, Southeast, Plains, Southwest, and Northwest. Brilliant colors, authentic photographs.

Petley Studios.

Publishes picture cards in color portraying Native American cultures. The photographs of children's faces, villages, dancers, and pottery artists are meaningful to young children.

Photographs of the Southwest. Photographs by Adam Clark Vroman. Ritchie, 1961.

Black and white full-page photographs include Hopi village scenes, women with squash blossom hairdress, Hopi blanket aritst, and Katchinatiku. Valuable addition to documentation of Southwest Indian groups.

Materials and Experiences

The Proof Press.

Request posters—"Indians: The First Americans," produced by John Zane. Anthropologist Albert B. Elsassu claims these portraits are accurate and are the most sympathetic renditions of American Indians ever produced. Prints represent original inhabitants of North America: Arctic, Northwest Coast, Plateau, California, Southwest, and Plains Indians.

Records

Authentic Indian Dances and Folklore with Carole Howard. Produced by Kimbo Educational. Distributed by Educational Activities. Album #9070.

Chippewas Eli Thomas and Issac Pelcher supply historical background that adds to the appreciation of these famous dances: Corn Grinder's Dance, the Rain Dance, the War Dance, and the Strawberry Dance. Manual is helpful. Craft projects, dance descriptions, symbols, and instructions for making instruments are included.

Canyon Records.

Records, cassettes, transparencies, study guides, photographs, maps, and bibliography about the Native American. Includes dances, tribal songs, and chants from numerous nations. Request catalog.

The Eskimos of Hudson Bay and Alaska. Produced by Folkways Records and Service Corporation. Distributed by Folkways Scholastic Records. Record #FE4444.

Authentic Eskimo songs for playing games, dancing, and hunting. Recorded on Hudson Bay by Laura Boulton and the residents of that area.

Indian Songs of the Southwest. Thunderbird Records. Record #TBR-1943B.

The music of Southwest Native Americans is related to their religion and life. Children create dances to this music.

Rabbit and the Fox. *Around the World in Dance: A Collection of Folk Dances for Early Childhood,* with Simon Williams. Distributed by Educational Activities.

Recording for this dance was done by a Chippewa Indian, chanting and playing authentic Chippewa instruments. Book of instructions accompanies records.

Shee-nasha. *Little Johnny Brown,* with Ella Jenkins. Distributed by Scholastic Records.

A Navajo song taught to Ella Jenkins by children on the Navajo Reservation in Arizona. Children learn this quickly.

Songs from the Pima. Canyon Records, 1970.

Social songs from the Pima groups include "Evening Song," "Blue Swallows," "Mountain Song," "Papago Park Mountain," sung to the beat of a drum.

Sounds of Indian America: Plains and Southwest. Distributed by Indian House. Record #87557.

Variety of music from several tribes has been recorded. Includes booklet that has large photographs and describes dances.

Films/Filmstrips

Clark, Ann Nolan. **Along Sandy Trails.** Baker & Taylor, 1975.

Filmstrip with cassette or record. Papago Indian girl and grandmother take a walk in the desert.

Native American Arts. Distributed by Modern Talking Picture Service.

A panoramic survey of the development of Native American artists and their works from prehistoric to contemporary times.

Navajo Film and Media Commission. Navajo Tribe.

Request list of films available for young children.

The Question That You Ask. Native American Solidarity Committee.

This 35-minute slide-tape presentation deals with the struggles Native Americans have faced in maintaining self-determination. An excellent source for adult awareness.

The Teepee: How It Is Made and Used. *The Plains Indians.* Produced by ACI Media. Distributed by Paramount Communications.

"The Teepee" filmstrip (35 mm — #510061) should be narrated by adult without the cassette. Filmstrip gives glimpse of family lodge as the basis of village life. Children learn about food, clothing, religion, artifacts, and customs. Set of four filmstrips for grades 4-7. "The Mandans" filmstrip is unacceptable for use with young children. Use of war paint and derogatory remarks about Sioux Indians are offensive. "The Buffalo and the Plains Indians" is repetitive and too slow-moving for young children.

Unlearning "Indian" Stereotypes. The Racism and Sexism Resource Center for Educators, 1977.

A filmstrip and book of teaching suggestions for teachers and librarians designed to eliminate stereotypes and increase knowledge about Native American children and their lives. Excellent for older children.

We Are the Evidence of This Western Hemisphere. Produced by International Indian Treaty Council Information Office. Distributed by Native American Solidarity Committee.

People from various Native nations discuss their history and current concerns in an hour-long videotape. In-depth treatment of the topics stimulate adult discussion.

The White Dawn. Produced by Paramount. Distributed by American Film Co.

Documentary of Northern Canadian Eskimo. Culture has been preserved, and most of it is traditional. The film provides the viewer with an insight into daily activities of the nomadic group.

Brigham Young University. Educational Media Services.

Request 16 mm film rental catalog.

Slides

Travel Slides. Produced by Technicolor Corporation. Distributed by Slides Unlimited.

Request a catalog of available slides.

Dolls

Indian Tribes of the United States. Heritage House.

Distributes Oglala Sioux tribe dolls. Authentic, fully-dressed, seven-and-one-half-inch boy and girl dolls. Historical sketch included.

Materials and Experiences

Arts and Crafts

Hopi Silvercraft Cooperative Guild.

Studio and gallery where artists' work is displayed. Indian pottery, jewelry, books, rugs, and baskets are displayed and sold. Visitors have the opportunity to view artisans at work. Silver overlay technique is a Hopi art. Request brochure.

Indian Arts and Crafts Board. U.S. Department of the Interior.

Source Directory 1: Indian and Eskimo Organizations Marketing Native American Arts and Crafts. Revised and updated regularly.

The businesses in this directory are Native American owned and operated arts and crafts organizations that offer a wide variety of arts and crafts for sale. Several nonprofit organizations are included which work directly with specific Native American groups to develop products and markets. The majority of the businesses maintain retail shops. Names, addresses, and telephone numbers of businesses are arranged by state.

Source Directory 2: Indian and Eskimo Individuals Marketing Native American Arts and Crafts. Revised and updated regularly.

The sources listed in this directory are Native American arts and crafts businesses which are privately owned and operated by (1) Indian or Eskimo artisans who design, produce, and market their exclusive products, often in combination with the products of other Native Americans; or (2) Indian or Eskimo merchants who retail and/or wholesale authentic Native American arts and crafts products. The majority of the sources listed maintain retail shops. The names, addresses, telephone numbers, and a description of the types of arts and crafts in each business are arranged by state.

Native American Arts and Crafts of the United States. Bibliography 1. Indian Arts and Crafts Board, 1971. Available from U.S. Government Printing Office, Superintendent of Documents.

The selected readings are suggested as an introduction to the richly varied arts and crafts created from prehistoric to modern times by Native American peoples of the United States. Annotated. Grouped by geographic area; includes Eskimos.

Navajo Arts and Crafts Guild.

Purpose: "To better utilize the resources of the Navajo and Hopi Tribes and reservations; . . . to engage in the promotion, production and sale of Navajo crafts to assist the artists and crafts workers of the Navajo people to make an adequate livelihood at this type of work; . . . to assist Navajo craftsmen to develop and maintain high standards of excellency in workmanship and design in their products which are sold by the Guild. . . ."

Programs: "Craftsmen are at work in silver at the Window Rock headquarters, and supplies are available for silversmiths, weavers, and leather craftsmen who work at home. The crafts exhibit of the Navajo Tribal Fair is handled by the Guild. An annual exhibit is held at the Heart Museum in Phoenix, Arizona, and exhibits are organized at several state fairs."

Palms Trading Co.

Wholesale distributor of pottery, jewelry, woven pieces, Kachina dolls, and numerous Indian items. Request information on how to distinguish between Indian and non-Indian made items.

Museums

The following is a selected list illustrating types of available museums. The Southwest has many small museums from which young children can learn more about the history of Native Americans. Check your community and your state for others.

Klein, Barry T. **Reference Encyclopedia of the American Indian.** Vol. 1. 2nd ed. Todd, 1973.

Complete list of museums, monuments, and parks.

American Museum of Natural History.

Eskimo exhibits depict Central, Western, and Greenland Eskimo culture; many artifacts. The exhibit of Indians of the Northwest Coast features Northwest Coast and Pacific Indian artifacts.

Arizona State Museum.

Contains ninety-two cases of Southwestern archaeological and ethnographic material. Ethnographic collection includes arts and crafts of the Pueblo, Navajo, Apache, Pima, and Papago Indians.

Chicago Natural History Museum.

Seven exhibit halls devoted to the American Indian. Collections and exhibits cover prehistoric and living Indians (and Eskimos) from Alaska to Cape Horn.

Hopi Cultural Center Museum.

Area artists' contributions to arts/crafts dominate the museum. The research center contains the best of Hopi crafts.

Inter-American Indian Institute.

Conducts development programs for Indian communities, trains technical personnel, investigates cultures of extinct Indian groups, and provides information services. Maintains a museum that exhibits examples of the arts, industry, etc., of various Indian groups. Write for a publications list.

Julesberg Historical Museum.

Local Indian artifacts, presumably of the Brule Sioux, Cheyenne, and Arapaho nations.

Pete Kitchen Western Museum.

The museum, a replica of Pete Kitchen's stronghold, is built of sun-dried adobe; four large rooms and the chapel are filled with displays of historical items pertinent to the Southwest: examples of early Navajo weaving; pipes, beadwork, and painted skins; Apache medicine shirt; old Navajo jewelry.

Koshare Indian Art Museum.

Collection of Indian and Western art by Western painters; Indian pottery, baskets, rugs, dioramas, artifacts.

Robert H. Lowie Museum of Anthropology.

Exhibits installed on separate subjects each year, featuring: (1) California Ethnographic—majority of which are basketry items; larger collections are Klamath River tribes, especially the Yurok, Modoc, Maidu, Miwok, Pomo, and Cahuilla. (2) North American Indian—ethnographic collections of which the Eskimo and Aleut material is the largest and most important single collection.

Museum of Fine Arts. Division of the Museum of New Mexico.

Exhibit of Indian artifacts, sculptures, and paintings.

National Museum of Natural History.

Ten exhibit halls deal with the archaeology, ethnology, and technology of the world; arranged geographically. Also, a hall on Peoples of the World—Physical Anthropology.

Materials and Experiences

Navajo Tribal Museum.

Permanent exhibits deal with animals, Navajo history, religion, arts and crafts. Outside exhibits include a full-scale, completely furnished hogan, with adjoining cornfield and sheep corral, plus a small zoo housing many of the animals native to the Navajo Reservation. Bibliographies, articles, and information are available.

Slater Memorial Museum.

Northwest Indian collection featuring Eskimo tools, implements, clothing, and artifacts; Northwest Coast boats, fishing tackle, houses, totems, utensils, trade objects, and basketry of the Tlingit, Haida, Nootka, Klikitat, and Salish.

Southeast Museum of the North American Indian.

Prehistoric and contemporary art and artifacts: stone carving, pottery, metalwork, textiles, weapons, basketry, utensils.

Southern Plains Indian Museum and Craft Center.

Exhibits feature hide painting, metalwork, beadwork, featherwork, carving, and dioramas. Craft shop operated by the Indian Arts and Crafts Board.

U.S. Department of the Interior Museum.

Collections contain items of handicraft, tools, utensils, dress, art, etc., of Native Americans. Exhibits include: full-sized birch bark canoe, chief's headdress, three glass cases of Indian handicraft items, and other artifacts.

Woodard's Indian Arts.

Museum houses original Indian paintings including work by Beatien Yazz and Andy Tsinajinnie; Woodard collection of Indian arts and crafts. Kachina dolls, carvings, textiles, silver and ancient objects. Arts and crafts shop.

Ceremonials/Events

Marquis, Arnold. **A Guide to America's Indians.** University of Oklahoma Press, 1974.

Indian nations, reservations, museums, and ceremonials are explained. Includes suggestions for attending these places and events. The book is divided into regions, with addresses for all sources.

The following illustrate a few of the regional ceremonials and events listed in the book.

Southwest
Early March — Indian Dance Festival, St. John's Mission, Gila River Reservation, Arizona.
Late April — Intertribal Dances, University of New Mexico, Albuquerque, New Mexico.
Memorial Day — Malki Spring Festival, Morongo Reservation, California.
Third Week in July — All-Indian Celebration, Fallon, Nevada.
Third Saturday/Sunday in August — Annual Indian Market, Santa Fe, New Mexico.
Early September — Navajo Tribal Fair, Window Rock, Arizona.

Central
Evenings, All Summer, Beginning in June — Intertribal Ceremonies, Chicago Indian Center, Chicago, Illinois.
June 26-28 — Intertribal Exposition, El Reno, Oklahoma.
July 2-5 — All-Indian Powwow, Cannon Ball, North Dakota.
August 7-9 — Indian Fair and Powwow, Lower Brule, South Dakota.
Fourth Weekend after Labor Day — Annual American Indian Ceremonial Dance, Oklahoma City, Oklahoma.

Northwest
Mid-March — Indian Fair, Wapato, Washington.
Early April — Spring Powwow, Warm Springs, Oregon.
First Weekend in August — All American Indian Days, Sheridan, Wyoming.

Southeast

February 20-22 — Seminole Powwow, Seminole Reservation, Hollywood, Florida.

Late June until Labor Day — Cherokee Drama, "Unto These Hills," Cherokee, North Carolina.

Northeast

Second Weekend in July — Powwow, Lewiston, New York.

September 2-4 — Powwow, Southampton, Long Island, New York.

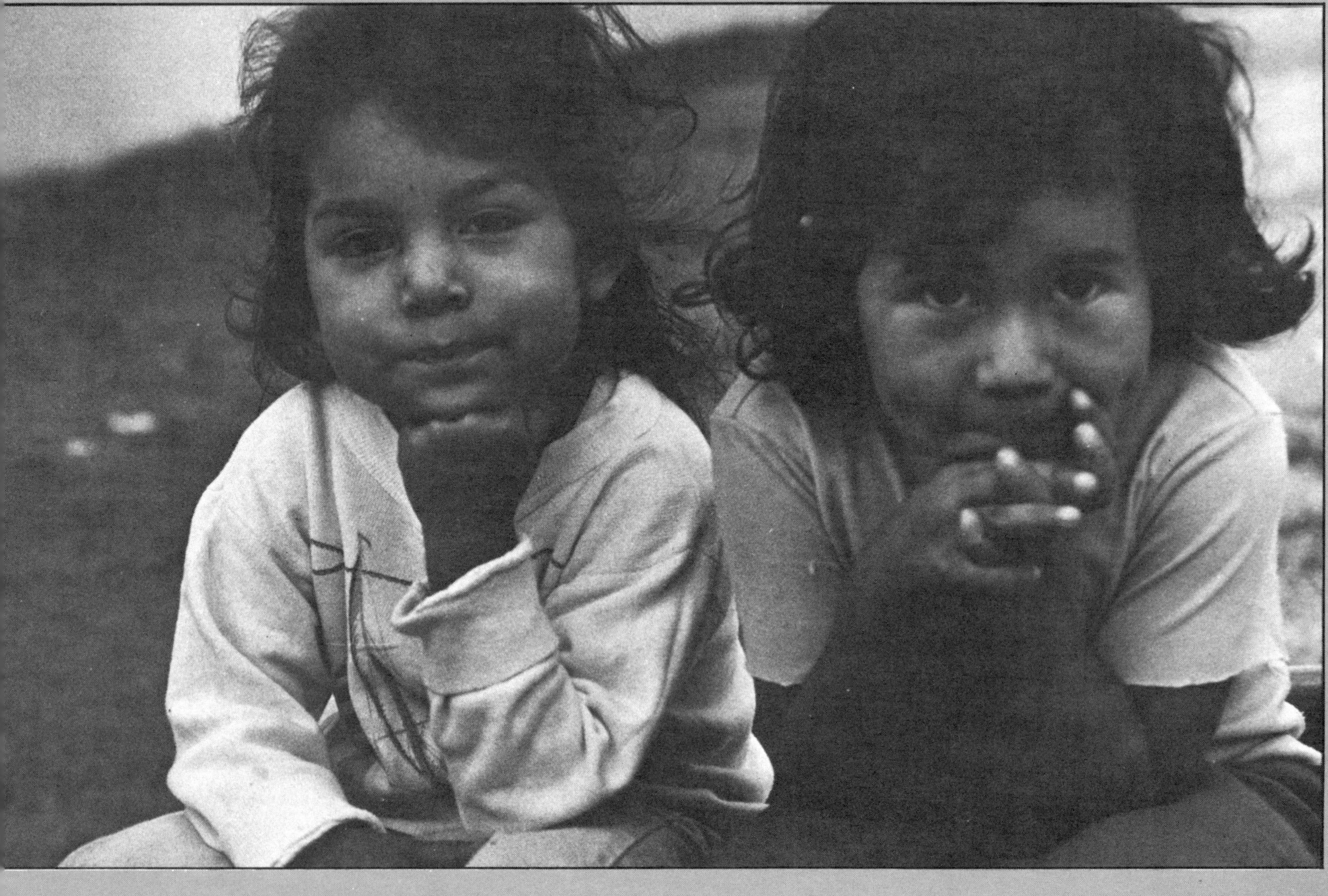
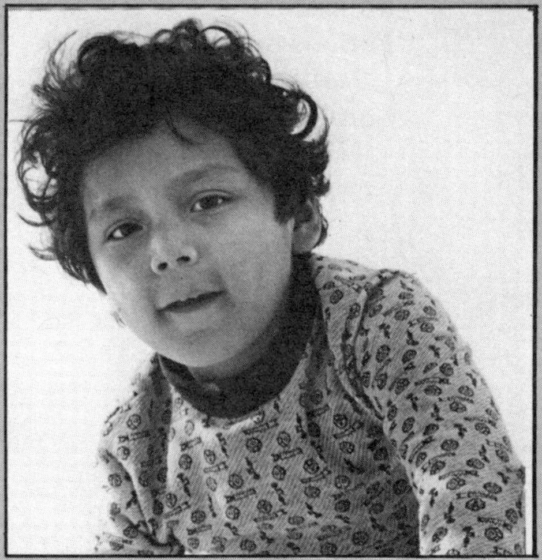
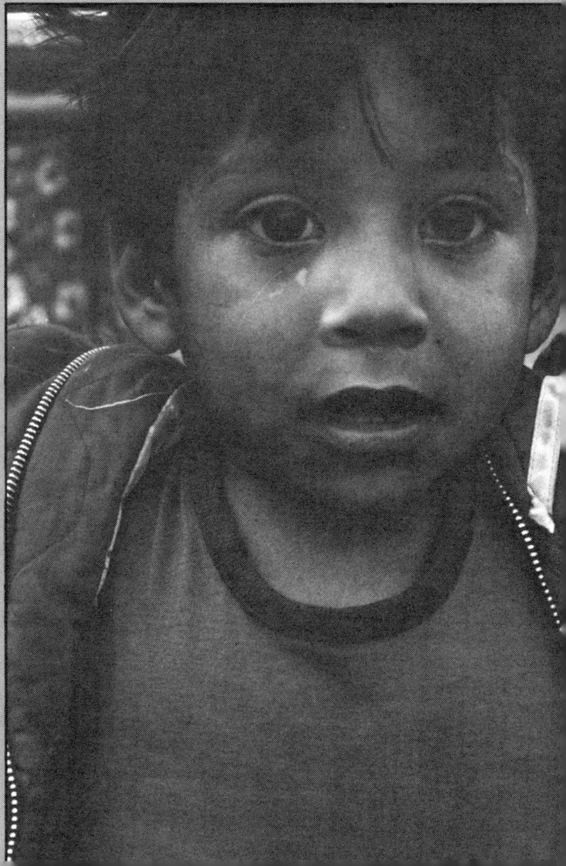

Spanish-Speaking Americans

Books for Children

ABC in English and Spanish. Lion, 1969. NK

Brilliant color illustrations by Robert Tallon of people, animals, and things that give the key to the meaning of the words. A bilingual pronunciation guide is provided for use by parents and teachers; however, check whether the Spanish dialect is that used in your community.

Albaum, Charlet. **Ojo de Dios: Eye of God.** Grosset and Dunlap, 1972. KPA

This handcraft was borrowed from ancient tradition of Pueblo and Mexican Indians. Book gives details for weaving various colored yarns onto sticks to make the Eye of God. Shapes and designs can be mastered by interested young children.

Anderson, Eloise A. **Carlos Goes to School.** Warne, 1973. KP

Carlos relates his adventure of his first day of school in a multicultural, informal environment. Subtle colors complement the text.

Archuleta, Nathaniel, dir. **Una Luminaria para Mis Palomitas; El Perrito Perdido; Perlitas de Ayer y Hoy; Ya Perdiste tu Colita, Tita.** Authors: Cecilia Apodaca, Nathaniel Archuleta, Olivia Martinez, Virginia Miera, Felipe Valerio. Distributed by Nathaniel Archuleta, University of New Mexico, 1975. NKP

Set of four books (three stories and a collection of poems, rhymes, and riddles) relevant to Chicano culture. Books are in Spanish with English instructions for adults. Choice of cassette tape or record with order.

Barry, Robert. **The Musical Palm Tree: A Story of Puerto Rico.** McGraw-Hill, 1965. KP

Line and wash drawings in shades of brown, green, and purple combine with the text to present San Juan, Puerto Rico, as shown to tourists guided by Pablito. He earns enough money to buy his mother a mantilla for the Fiesta Patronal.

Belpre, Pura. **Santiago.** Warne, 1969. KP

A Puerto Rican boy seeks to establish relationships in a new community, and sensitive friends offer him support. Provides a situation that reflects experiences of minority children. Art by Symeon Shimin adds to the mood of the book.

Bilingual ABC in Verse, ABECEDARIO Bilingue en Verso. Instructional Challenges, 1974. KP

In English and Spanish. Each letter in the alphabet is accompanied by a verse and suggested activities.

Blue, Rose. **I Am Here, Yo Estoy Aquí.** Watts, 1971. KP

A Puerto Rican child feels lonely in her American environment. Illustrates the importance of bilingual education. One of the few books written in English for children tuned to language difficulty of the Spanish-speaking child.

Spanish-Speaking Americans

Brenner, Barbara. **Caras (Faces).** Spanish version by Alma Flor Ada. Dutton, 1977. KP

Two eyes, two ears, a nose—a face. Everybody has one, yet we all look different and we each see, sense, and react in different ways. Illustrated with photographs.

Camille, Josephine. **Carlos and the Brave Owl.** Random House, 1968. KP

Carlos has no pet to participate in the Blessing of the Animals. What happens when Carlos finds an owl? Bright-colored illustrations and text can be read to or by young children.

Carlson, Vada F. **High Country.** Northland, 1972. KP

Poetry that can be read to young children. Illustrations by Joe Rodriguez enhance and complement the poems. "The Desert Speaks" and "Desert Picture" are special poems for young children. In English.

Cooper, Lee. **Fun with Spanish.** Little, Brown, 1969. KP

Written in English with some Spanish words. This elementary Spanish book can be read by some children. Adult can use words for labeling. Dictionary includes lists of proper names, color words, and animals.

Dines, Glen. **Sun, Sand and Steel: Costumes and Equipment of the Spanish/Mexican Southwest.** Putnam's, 1972. KP

Brilliant, colorful illustrations of serapes, vests, mochilas, flags, armas, chaparejos. Text for older children.

Ets, Marie Hall. **Gilberto and the Wind.** Viking, 1963. KN

Gilberto experiences the wind as both a friend and an enemy. Children can "read the story" from the pictures. Effective illustrations but minimal cultural references. In English.

Fern, Eugene. **Lorenzo and Angelina.** Farrar, Straus and Giroux, 1968. KP

Adventures of Angelina and her donkey have appeal for children. Enjoyable when read in dialog form. Illustrated by colorful and detailed drawings. Uses some Spanish.

Frasconi, Antonio. **The Snow and the Sun.** Harcourt Brace Jovanovich, 1961. KP

A South American folk rhyme written in English and Spanish. Illustrated with exciting, bold, and colorful Frasconi woodcuts. The rhyme emphasizes that everything in nature is related to something else and that each act has its consequences.

Glubok, Shirley. **The Art of Ancient Mexico.** Harper & Row, 1968. KP

These photographs of art from ancient Mexican civilizations are enticing to children. Similar clay and pottery figures may be viewed in museums.

Goldberg, Martha. **Big House, Little House.** Scholastic Book Services, 1971. K

Stories about secrets intrigue young children. A young Mexican boy seeks to preserve the image of his beautiful friend.

Goldin, Augusta. **Pelo Lacio, Pelo Rizo.** Crowell, 1968. KP

Translation of the story "Straight Hair, Curly Hair." Children become aware of how people have different types of hair.

Grifalconi, Ann. **The Toy Trumpet.** Bobbs-Merrill, 1968. KP

Tomas dreams, waits, saves, and finally gets his wish. The story is laced with Spanish words. Children identify with Tomas and his fantasy. Unusual and pleasing use of colors.

Books for Children

Hall, Adelaide. **The Runaway Hat.** Singer, 1969. KP

    Large book, simple text. Vividly illustrated by Marilyn Hirsh. The story of Carlos and the loss of his straw hat. In English.

Hampton, Doris. **Just for Manuel.** Steck-Vaughn, 1971. NKP

    This story shows the need of a child for his very own place, as Manuel searches for a place of his own in his family's crowded apartment. Children respond to this story. In English.

Hancock, Sibyl. **Mario's Mystery Machine.** Putnam's, 1972. KP

    Mario's construction is a secret. Spanish words are introduced in this "see and read" book. Tomie de Paola's illustrations add appeal to the book. In English.

Hitte, Kathryn, and W. D. Hayes. **Mexicali Soup.** Parents' Magazine Press, 1970. KP

    Mama's special Mexicali soup is diluted by family members because each feels that her/his family "should do what others do here." The story conveys the message that to dilute one's culture may mean to lose it. In English.

Hood, Flora. **One Luminaria for Antonio.** Putnam's, 1966. KP

    A story about a small boy and his family at Christmastime. Portrays the Christmas customs of midnight mass and luminarias. In English.

Jenness, Aylette, and L. W. Kroeber. **A Life of Their Own: An Indian Family in Latin America.** Crowell, 1975. KP

    A Guatemalan family gives insight into Indian culture as revealed through daily activities of agriculture, transportation, education, religion, and craft work. The text is for older children and adults, but the photographs interest young children. In English, Spanish glossary is provided.

Joslin, Sesyle, and J. Alcorn. **La Fiesta.** Harcourt Brace Jovanovich, 1967. KP

    A story about a fiesta. In Spanish only. Colorful and large type.

Joslin, Sesyle, and K. Barry. **There Is a Bull in My Balcony/Hay un Toro en Mi Balcón.** Harcourt Brace Jovanovich, 1966. KP

    A tongue-in-cheek tour of Mexico through useful phrases in Spanish and English.

Kern, Ann. **Two Pesos for Catalina.** Scholastic Book Services, 1967. KP

    Discerning Catalina goes on an adventure to spend silver money. The book involves children in the excitement of making choices. Spanish names and words can expand vocabularies.

Krumgold, Joseph. **And Now Miguel.** Crowell, 1953. KP

    Miguel, son of a New Mexican shepherd, longs to be old enough to go with the men to take the sheep to summer pasture. Film available from Universal-Education and Visual Arts.

Langner, Nola. **Joseph and the Wonderful Tree.** Addison-Wesley, 1975. KP

    Not relevant to the Mexican cultural experience, although the language is Spanish and the setting is Mexico. Langner, who lives in a lighthouse, gives an excellent and humorous perspective on the serious nature of hostility.

Lexau, Joan. **María.** Dial, 1964. NKP

    A story in English about how a Puerto Rican girl in New York City finally gets a doll, even though money is scarce.

Marcus, Rebecca B. **Fiesta Time in Mexico.** Garrard, 1974. KPA

Photographs of the nacimiento, posada, and numerous celebrations of interest to young children. An excellent resource for adults and older children. In English.

Martel, Cruz. **Yagua Days.** Dial, 1976. NKP

A story that gains children's attention with its adventure of a young Puerto Rican American, Adan, who learns that yagua days are special days. Embellished with Spanish words and phrases, the book provides insight about Puerto Rican culture. In English, Spanish glossary is included.

Mistral, Gabriela. **Crickets and Frogs.** Atheneum, 1972. KP

Translated and adapted by Doris Dana, this fable is a part of the heritage of many Latin American children. In Spanish and English.

Mistral, Gabriela. **The Elephant and His Secret.** Atheneum, 1974. K

Set in Uruguay, this fable tells of the adventures of the elephant as he makes his way in the world. In Spanish and English. Illustrated in bold woodcuts.

Nash, Veronica. **Carlito's World: A Block in Spanish Harlem.** McGraw-Hill, 1969. NK

Few books explore Puerto Rican sections in New York. This one stereotypes—Puerto Ricans fighting, girls sitting and reading passively while boys explore—but displays positive family relationships. In English.

Nims, Bonnie. **Yo Quisiera Vivir en un Parque de Juegos: I Wish I Lived at the Playground.** Translated by Ramón S. Orellana. O'Hara Publishers, 1972. NK

Childhood experiences on a seesaw, on a swing, in a sandpile, and playing Hide and Seek, with Chicano, Black, and White children. In English and Spanish.

Politi, Leo. **Juanita.** Scribner's, 1948. P

Juanita celebrates her fourth birthday on Olivera Street in old Los Angeles. Spanish names, songs, and phrases enable young children to experience the culture and lifestyle of a small traditional Mexican-American community. In English. Recommended by a Chicano teacher.

Politi, Leo. **Pedro el Angel de la Calle Olivera.** Scribner's, 1974. **Pedro—The Angel of Olivera Street.** Scribner's, 1946. KP

Some Mexican Americans protest that this book stereotypes their culture while others regard this story as a classic for Christmastime. What is your evaluation?

Prieto, Mariana B. **Johnny Lost, Juanito Perdido.** Day, 1969. NKP

In English and Spanish. Johnny moves from Puerto Rico to the United States, where he gets lost and has problems communicating his needs. Johnny makes several friends from different ethnic backgrounds. This is a helpful book to start a discussion on friendship or communication.

Rider, Alex. **When We Go to Market, Cuando Vamos al Mercado.** Funk and Wagnalls, 1969.

A bilingual "learn-a-language" picture book. Children learn the words for many items in the market.

Rockwell, Anne. **El Toro Pinto and Other Songs in Spanish.** Macmillan, 1971. KP

The thirty Spanish songs include guitar accompaniment and translations. Accurately researched pictures illustrate the costumes, plants, architecture, and animals appropriate to each song. Songs reflect the mood of Mexico, but the rhythms and melodies come from many cultures.

Rowland, Florence W. **School for Julio.** Putnam's, 1968. KP

A story about how a school comes to a small village in Mexico. Good example of the self-help concept utilized by the villagers.

Books for Children

Scarry, Richard. **Mi Primer Gran Libro para Leer.** Larousse, 1975. KP

   A picture book translated from English which elicits many comments and questions. Several other Richard Scarry books in Spanish are available from Larousse and International Learning Systems. Useful for learning Spanish words.

Serfozo, Mary. **Welcome, Roberto! ¡Bienvenido, Roberto!** Follett, 1969. KP

   Roberto's world includes an informal integrated classroom. Book includes bilingual text and large black and white photographs.

Dr. Seuss. **The Cat in the Hat Beginner Book Dictionary in Spanish.** Random House, 1966. NKP

   Can be used as a reading or reference book.

Simon, Norma. **What Do I Say?/¿Qué Digo?** Whitman, 1967. KP

   An English/Spanish version with large pictures and few words, including basic phrases such as "good morning" and "buenos dias," which are helpful for learning either Spanish or English. Simon's book *What Do I Do?* has also been translated into Spanish—*¿Qué Hago?*

Sonneborn, Ruth. **Friday Night Is Papa Night.** Viking, 1970. KP

   Illustrations and text depict a loving family coping with a poverty situation. Papa's two jobs allow him to come home only on Friday, but one night he is late. In English.

Sonneborn, Ruth. **Seven in a Bed.** Viking, 1968. NKP

   A warm story of a Puerto Rican family on their first day in New York. With the added nieces and nephews, there is much confusion until Papa gets all the children settled. In English.

Storm, Dan. **Picture Tales from Mexico.** Lippincott, 1941. KP

   Children delight in Mexican folktales such as "The Race Between the Rabbit and the Frog" and "The Wax Doll."

Talbot, Toby. **Coplas: Folk Poems in Spanish and English.** Four Winds, 1972. NKP

   Collection of short improvised verses. Comic and tragic, these songs in English and Spanish express feelings about work, play, people, life, death, and nature. Incites young children to create verses of their own. Impressionable woodcuts by Rocco Negri.

Talbot, Toby. **Two by Two.** Follett, 1974. NK

   From the hairless-as-a-pig armadillo to a zebra who stalks the African plains, this bilingual alphabet book by a Spanish teacher is of interest to young children. Descriptive sketches.

Thomas, Dawn C. **¡Mira! ¡Mira!** Lippincott, 1970. KP

   A boy from Puerto Rico comes to New York and, for the first time, experiences an exciting plane ride, an elevator ride up fourteen floors, and fun in the snow. Illustrated with line drawings.

Todd, Barbara. **Juan Patricio.** Putnam's, 1972. KP

   Juan, in Santa Fe, wants a job since everyone in his family has one. He tries many things unsuccessfully but finally a puppy comes to his rescue. In English.

U.S. Committee for United Nations Children's Fund. **Mexico.** Hi Neighbor. Hastings House, 1961. KP

   Fourth book in a series. Introduces children to stories, songs, recipes, clothes, festivals, and toys from Mexico.

Vavra, Robert. **Pizorro.** Harcourt Brace Jovanovich, 1968. KP

   Actual moments with piñata, with a burro, and in a market make Pizorro's rural life special and rich in the "bounties and beauties of nature."

Warren, Betsy. **Papacito and His Family.** Steck-Vaughn, 1969. NKP

    Saturated with Spanish words, the story describes Beto's day. Pictures and glossary are helpful. Illustrations stereotype the Mexican with sombreros and shawls. In English.

Weiner, Sandra. **Small Hands, Big Hands: Profiles of Chicano Migrant Workers and Their Families.** Pantheon, 1970. KP

    Adult resource with information about Mexican migrant families. Children respond to the full-page photographs.

Williams, Barbara. **El Dolor de Muelas de Alberto (Albert's Toothache).** Spanish version by Alma Flor Ada. Dutton, 1977. NKP

    Albert Turtle is sure he has a toothache, but no one believes him. Then grandmother comes to visit — and knows exactly what to do. Albert's problem is familiar to children in any language.

Williams, Letty. **The Tiger!/¡El Tigre!** Prentice-Hall, 1970. KP

    A folktale in English and Spanish in which Maria and her dog outwit a Latin American jaguar. Illustrations are bright and humorous. The story of "The Little Red Hen" has also been translated into Spanish by Letty Williams and is available from Prentice-Hall.

Williamson, Shelagh. **Pepi's Bell.** Singer, 1969. K

    Adventures of a burro in Mexico as he attempts to escape responsibility. Illustrations by Patricia Combs are appealing to young children. In English.

Resources for Adults

Books and Articles

Advisory Committee on Education of Spanish and Mexican Americans.

An arm of the United States Office of Education, this committee advises the Commissioner of Education on policies for programs on education of Mexican Americans, Cuban Americans, Puerto Rican Americans, and other Spanish-speaking persons.

Alurista. **Floricanto en Aztlan.** Chicano Cultural Center, 1971.

Literature and the arts are the most intimate reflection of human growth over time. With this principle, the Chicano Cultural Center introduces the Creative Series for the works of Chicano artists of importance and influence in the current cultural renaissance of the Chicano people.

Anderson, Theodore, and M. Boyer. **Bilingual Schooling in the United States.** 2 vols. Southwest Educational Development Laboratory, 1970.

An excellent source of information for the extent and location of bilingual education in the United States, contains excellent materials facilitating the establishment of such programs.

Brady, Agnes M. **La Navidad.** National Textbook, 1970.

A collection of Christmas customs, songs, plays, and poems from Mexico, Latin America, and Spain.

Bravo-Villasante, Carmen. **Antología de la Literatura Infantil Lengua Española.** 2 vols. Doncel, 1973.

The two volumes comprise a collection of children's literature in the Spanish language. A resource for the bilingual teacher, to tell or read the stories in either Spanish or English.

Bravo-Villasante, Carmen. **Antología de la Literatura Infantil Universal.** 2 vols. Doncel, 1971.

An anthology of stories to be told to children, compiled by an international authority on children's literature for the Spanish-speaking world. Useful for the bilingual teacher.

Cabrera, Y. Arturo. **Emerging Faces: The Mexican-Americans.** Brown, 1971.

A short study dealing with major issues in Mexican-American studies: education, housing, politics, literature, religion, Chicano identity. The discussion of the treatment of Mexican Americans in children's literature is particularly useful.

Carter, Thomas P. **Mexican Americans in School: A History of Education Neglect.** College Entrance Examination Board, 1970.

A sad picture of the poor quality of education and the neglect of the basic needs of Mexican Americans in America.

Castañeda, Alfredo, M. Ramirez III, and P. Herold. **New Approaches to Bilingual, Bicultural Education.** Dissemination and Assessment Center for Bilingual Bicultural Education, 1975.

A book of teacher-training materials based on the philosophy of "cultural democracy." This philosophy recognizes the individuality of both students and teachers. Through independent self-paced instruction, teachers can evaluate their techniques and the learning styles of the children.

Chicano History, 450 Years of Chicano History. Chicano Studies, University of New Mexico.

A bilingual pictorial history of 176 pages with 566 pictures.

Coy, Harold. **Chicano Roots Go Deep.** Dodd, Mead, 1975.

Chicano history that intermingles truths and insights as well as stereotypes and distortions. By covering socioeconomic and artistic areas, the author helps the reader appreciate the diversity of Chicano culture and life, especially the relationship between the Chicanos and Mexicans. Grade 7 and up.

Cordasco, Francesco, and E. Bucchioni. **The Puerto Rican Community and Its Children on the Mainland.** Scarecrow, 1972.

Articles about the Puerto Rican culture, the family, and the experiences of Puerto Rican children in North American schools.

Directory of Title VII ESEA Bilingual Education Programs: 1975-76. Dissemination and Assessment Center for Bilingual Bicultural Education, 1976.

The fourth annual directory of ESEA-funded programs during the 1975-76 school year. The 406 grants were awarded to instructional, teacher-education, institutional development, and service programs in 38 states and territories, and in 47 languages. Programs are described. The address of each program enables the reader to write for additional information.

Epstein, Sam, and B. Epstein. **The First Book of Mexico.** Watts, 1967.

The section on "Bread of Mexico" is useful when preparing tortillas with children. Photographs.

Fergusson, Erna. **Mexican Cookbook.** University of New Mexico Press, 1970.

Authentic recipes for famous Mexican dishes. Old Mexican recipes have been adapted for American kitchens. An oft-revised book since 1934; a classic sourcebook.

Galarza, Ernesto. **Spiders in the House and Workers in the Field.** University of Notre Dame Press, 1970.

Gives the lay person an understanding of the plight of the farmworker as well as a knowledge of Mexican Americans.

Galarza, Ernesto, and others. **Mexican-Americans in the Southwest.** McNally and Loftin, 1969.

Surveys the effects of farm mechanization, urban redevelopment, population squeeze, and other root causes of upheaval on Mexican-American communities in California, Texas, Arizona, New Mexico, and Colorado. Traces the immigration movement. The authors assess the current economic, political, cultural, and educational status of the Spanish-speaking people of the Southwest and project the form and direction of growth of the nation's second largest minority.

Gonzales, Jorge, ed. **El Ombligo de Aztlan.** Center of Chicanos Studies Publications, 1971.

The poetry was written by Chicano students from Chicano creative writing classes, members of the Toltecans en Aztlan, and members of a Chicano artist organization.

Resources for Adults

Grebler, Leo, J. W. Moore, and R. C. Guzmán. **The Mexican-American People: The Nation's Second Largest Minority.** Free Press, 1970.

A monumental work on Mexican Americans resulting from over four years of research. Using original data, the authors discuss major facets of Mexican-American life: education, labor, immigration, religion, housing, family structure, socialization, and acculturation. The diversities within the Mexican-American culture are stressed. Extensive, unannotated bibliography included.

Hernandez, Luis. **A Forgotten American.** Anti-Defamation League of B'nai B'rith, 1970.

A resource unit for teachers on the Mexican American.

Holman, Rosemary. **Spanish Nuggets.** Naylor, 1968.

A collection of "dichos" or Mexican sayings in Spanish with English translations. An attractive book—printed on tan paper with brown wash illustrations.

Hubp, Loretta B. **Let's Play Games in Spanish I.** National Textbook, 1968.

Some of the games, skits, and teacher aids for helping non-Spanish speakers learn some Spanish words may be suitable for younger children.

Illinois Advisory Committee. **Equal Education: A Right; Igualdad en la Educación: Un Derecho.** U.S. Commission on Civil Rights, 1976.

A handbook for parents who want to know more about bilingual-bicultural education. In Spanish and English. Order Item #288-A.

Information and Materials to Teach the Cultural Heritage of the Mexican American Child. Dissemination and Assessment Center for Bilingual Bicultural Education, 1974.

A bilingual reference book for background information and materials to guide children into a cultural awareness of Mexican heritage. Celebrations; arts and crafts; Mexican foods; poems, songs, and games; dances; and legends, fables, and stories are included.

John, Vera P., and V. Horner. **Early Childhood Bilingual Education.** Modern Language Association of America, 1971.

Descriptions of bilingual programs for Spanish-speaking and Native American children from kindergarten through grade three. Addresses of programs are included so the reader can secure additional information. Lists of bilingual publications and bilingual materials available from various publishers with addresses; records also included.

Jones, Edward H., Jr., and M. S. Jones. **Arts and Crafts of the Mexican People.** Ritchie, 1971.

Old crafts of the Indians are produced in old ways today as well as through modern day techniques.

Main, Margaret H. **Olé Days for Your Classroom.** *Early Years* 6 (October 1975): 23-25.

Numerous ideas for activities that explore Chicano culture. Documented by photographs of children making rebozos, playing Jicotillo, learning to count, breaking piñatas, and making tacos.

Manuel, Herschel T. **Spanish Speaking Children of the Southwest: Their Education and the Public Welfare.** University of Texas Press, 1965.

Shows lack of education as a primary cause of poverty. Language deficiency and cultural deprivation of long-continued poverty is often unbearable. Letters from Spanish-speaking students tell of difficulties experienced in English-speaking schools.

McWilliams, Carey. **Ill Fares the Land: Migrants and Migratory Labor in the United States.** Little, Brown, 1967.

A historic description of the process of land migration and the labor exodus westward in the United States.

McWilliams, Carey. **North from Mexico, the Spanish Speaking People of the United States.** Greenwood, 1968. (Reprint of the 1949 edition.)

A classic work concerning Mexican Americans in the United States. This book also deals with the history of the Southwest and the conflicts between the two cultures.

Mexican American Studies Program. University of Houston.

Carries out research and instructional activities dealing with Mexican-American issues, sociology, education, and language. Also provides instruction in ethnic studies in the area of Mexican-American relations.

Moreno, Stephen. **Parents-Padres-Teach Your Children to Learn.** Moreno Education Co.

Seven Spanish-English booklets that encourage parents to take an active role in child's learning experiences from childhood to adolescence.

Newlon, Clarke. **Famous Mexican Americans.** Dodd, Mead, 1972.

A compilation of brief biographies of prominent Mexican Americans. Includes material on Henry Ramirez (educator), Lee Trevino (golfer), Cesar Chavez (labor leader), Anthony Quinn (actor), Ricardo Montalban (actor), Henry B. Gonzalez (U.S. congressional representative), Joe Kapp (professional football player), Joseph Montoya (former U.S. senator), Vikki Carr (entertainer), Reies Tijerina (visionary), Hilary Sandoval (business executive), Trini Lopez (entertainer), Pancho Gonzales (professional tennis player), Lupe Anguiano (educator), and others.

Ortego, Philip D. **We Are Chicanos: An Anthology of Mexican-American Literature.** Washington Square, 1973.

A collection including poetry, drama, and fiction, along with essays on Mexican-American background, folklore, and "the movement." A short bibliography is provided.

Paredes, Americo, and R. Paredes. **Mexican-American Authors.** Houghton Mifflin, 1972.

A collection of folklore, stories, essays, poems, and one play by Mexican Americans. The anthology places an emphasis on folklore in the Mexican-American literary tradition and provides an overview of the development of Mexican-American writing in the last fifty years.

Partners in Language: A Guide for Parents; Compañeros en el Idioma: Guia para los Padres. American Speech and Hearing Association.

Free book offering suggestions to parents in area of language development. In Spanish and English.

Prieto, Mariana, col. **Play It in Spanish.** Day, 1973. Music by Elizabeth C. Nielsen.

Spanish games and folksongs for children. Mariana Prieto collected folklore in her travels in Latin American countries, the West Indies, Mexico, and Spain. Each folksong is identified by country. Words in English and Spanish with music accompaniment.

Puerto Rican History, Civilization and Culture: A Mini-Documentary. Bilingual Unit of the New York State Department of Education, 1973. Distributed by Dissemination and Assessment Center for Bilingual Bicultural Education.

The book deals with various aspects of Puerto Rican life. Sources of information for further study range from novels to scholarly research.

Resources for Adults

Quirarte, Jacinto. **Mexican American Artists.** University of Texas Press, 1973.

    Information about Mexican-American artists who depict the Chicano/Spanish-speaking cultures.

Ramirez, Manuel, III. **Bilingual Education as a Vehicle for Institutional Change.** *Mexican Americans and Educational Change,* ed. Alfredo Castañeda and others. Arno, 1974.

    Ramirez states that if Mexican-American children are to maintain identity with their ethnic heritage while adapting to the values and lifestyles of mainstream America, then fundamental changes in curriculum and teaching strategies must be made.

Ramirez, Manuel, III. **Introduction, Part V.** *Cultural Democracy: The Challenge of Bilingual Education,* ed. Alfredo Castañeda and others. Arno, 1974.

    The main theme of this introduction is that the success or failure of bicultural-bilingual education may determine whether cultures whose values and lifestyles differ from those of the mainstream American middle class will be allowed representation in American education.

Ramirez, Manuel, III. **Potential Contributions by the Behavioral Sciences to Effective Preparation Programs for Teachers of Mexican-American Children.** *Educating the Mexican American,* ed. Henry Sioux and William J. Hernandez-M. Judson, 1970.

    The contribution of research in the behavioral sciences has identified the value orientation of the Mexican-American culture. Adults who work with children should use this information in relating to Mexican-American children and in planning programs for them.

Ramirez, Manuel, III, and A. Castañeda. **Cultural Democracy, Bicognitive Development and Education.** Academic, 1974.

    This book is concerned with how American society can promote and sustain its diversity and be sensitive to individual differences through educational pluralism. The philosophy of "cultural democracy" assumes that people have a legal and moral right to remain identified with their own ethnic group, values, language, home, and community as they learn and accept "mainstream" values. Attention is focused on Mexican Americans. The appendixes include valuable aids for assessing cognitive styles, field independent/field sensitive instruments for observing behavior of children and teachers, and recommendations for culture-matching teaching strategies.

Resource Centers.

    Title VII centers provide information on bilingual-bicultural education.
The Bilingual Education Service Center.
Bilingual/Bicultural Resource Center.
Bilingual Education Resource Center.

Shular, Antonia, and others. **Literature Chicano Texto y Contexto.** Prentice-Hall, 1971.

    This imaginative anthology of Chicano literature presents popular corridos and folktales, by poets, novelists, students, migrant workers, and prisoners in federal penitentiaries, as well as an Aztec king, a nun in colonial Mexico, and a modern Mexican proponent of "La Raza Cósmica." All provide eloquent testimony to the Chicano experience.

Stone, Idella. **Thirty Mexican Menus in Spanish and English.** Ritchie, 1971.

    A bilingual book of recipes.

Toor, Frances. **A Treasury of Mexican Folkways.** Crown, 1947.

    Myths, customs, folklore, traditions, beliefs, fiestas, dances, and songs of the Mexican culture. A comprehensive resource.

Waters, Frank. **People of the Valley.** Swallow, 1969.

    A moving story of one of the most powerful Spanish-speaking peoples of the Southwest who were almost in a foreign land. Within the United States they confronted a threatening world of change.

Willes, Burlington. **Games and Ideas for Teaching Spanish.** Fearon, 1967.

Games and ideas increase learning motivation through oral communication skills and cultural enrichment in a stimulating spirit of play. Particularly for children in the primary grades.

Bibliographies

Barrios, Ernie, and others, comps. **Bibliographía de Aztlan: An Annotated Chicano Bibliography.** Center of Chicanos Studies Publications, 1971.

An annotated, topically-arranged bibliography that includes more than 300 books and articles published between 1920 and 1971.

A Bibliography of Bilingual-Bicultural Preschool Materials for the Spanish Speaking Child. U.S. Department of Health, Education, and Welfare, Office of Child Development, 1977.

For teachers and paraprofessionals in early childhood programs serving Spanish-speaking children in the United States. Includes curriculum guides, instructional materials, and supplemental materials. Annotated. Also available from ERIC Document Reproduction Service, ED 142 045.

Bilingual Bicultural Materials: A Listing for Library Resource Centers. El Paso Schools, 1974 and 1975.

An annotated list of over 1,100 filmstrips, recordings, kits, games, and charts with recommendations. The materials were evaluated by teachers and librarians for bilingual and intercultural programs. Grade levels that range from K to 12 are designated for each item. Complete information for ordering is included. A separate publication for each year with different entries in each.

Cabello-Argandoña, Roberto, and others, eds. **The Chicana: A Comprehensive Bibliographic Study.** Chicano Studies Center, Bibliographic Research Division, Bibliographic Research and Collection Development Unit, 1976.

This volume is one of a series resulting from a bibliographic investigation concerned with compiling information pertaining to the Chicano experience. This annotated bibliography of films, journals, culture and cultural processes, and all major subject areas, is for adults.

California State University, Chicano Research Library. **Early Childhood Education: A Selected Bibliography.** Chicano Studies Center, 1972.

The first phase of mechanized search for materials on early childhood and the Chicano.

Centro de Estudios Puertorriqueños.

Center for information on Puerto Ricans and Puerto Rico. Collection of bilingual materials and films on history, culture, and the struggle for independence.

Chicano: A Selected Bibliography. Inland Library System, 1971.

Selected bibliography of English/Spanish language materials that reflects various points of view and "focuses upon contemporary interests and concerns of the Mexican-American community." Also includes publications of earlier generations of scholars concerned with the culture of Chicanos.

Chicanos Studies Library Project. Arizona State University.

Covers all subjects including bilingual education. Publishes annual bibliographies.

Conwell, Mary K., and P. Belpre. **Libros en Español: An Annotated List of Children's Books in Spanish.** New York Public Library, 1971.

Resources for Adults

Hill, Marnesba D., and H. B. Schleifer. **Puerto Rican Authors: A Bibliographic Handbook; Autores Puertorriqueños: Una Guia Bibliográfica.** Scarecrow, 1974.

This handbook, written by Puerto Rican authors, is a bilingual annotated bibliographical guide to the history and literature of Puerto Rico from 1493 to the present.

Hispanic-American Institute.

Works to make resources available for a greater understanding of, and service to, people of Hispanic culture in the United States and Latin America. Resources include leadership recruitment and training, continuing education programs for pastors, research projects and interpretive materials on the relationship of Christianity and Hispanic culture, and United States-Latin American interchange of educators and students. Publishes a biennial bibliographic guide.

Institute for Cultural Pluralism. San Diego State University, School of Education.

The ICP Resource Center provides review and research of materials. There are 36,000 education materials available for purchase. Bibliography is being computerized. At present Spanish is the only language included; however, provisions are being made to provide materials in Asian and Native American languages.

Institute of Latin American Studies.

Internationally recognized as one of the major centers for the study of Latin America, the institute's mission is educational. The institute's bulletin provides information concerning its resources, activities, and personnel.

Mexican Americans. Xerox Book Catalogs Department.

A ninety-page bibliography of books, filmstrips, records, tapes, and periodicals for children and adults.

Nogales, Luis G., and others, eds. **The Mexican American: A Selected and Annotated Bibliography.** Center for Latin American Studies, Stanford University, 1971.

A revised and enlarged bibliography of 444 entries oriented toward sociological studies of the Mexican American; includes citations of sociological studies of a theoretical nature. The most useful bibliography for students interested in a sociological approach.

Proyecto Leer Bulletin.

Evaluates and reviews educational materials in Spanish and ethnic literature in English. Annotations are informative as well as critical. Bulletin also features reviews of records, periodicals, and special materials for adult basic education, as well as recommendations of books and nonprint materials for children and adults.

Special Issue on Chicano Materials. *Interracial Books for Children Bulletin* 5, nos. 7 and 8 (1975). Council on Interracial Books for Children.

Special feature is the survey of 200 books on Chicano themes. All the old favorites are included with criteria for careful selection of books. Lists recommended adult books.

Trejo, Arnulfo D. **Bibliografía Chicano: Books by, about, and for Chicanos,** with an Introductory Essay. Gale Research, 1975.

A selected, annotated bibliography of books and monographs on Chicanos, with the scope of the bibliography from 1848 to the present. The listing is topical, covering a broad range of subjects. Contains a list of Chicano periodicals and an author and title index.

Valdez, Armando, ed. **Directorio Chicano.** Southwest Network, 1976.

Lists names and addresses of Chicano research centers, publishers, distributors and booksellers, journals and magazines, newsletters, newspapers, film producers, and film distributors.

Vivo, Paquita, ed. **The Puerto Ricans: An Annotated Bibliography.** Bowker, 1973.

    The first English bibliography compiled by the Puerto Rican Research and Resources Center. Includes Puerto Rican history, folklore, the arts, juvenile literature, periodicals, audio-visual materials, and many other topics.

Words Like Freedom. California Association of School Librarians.

    An annotated bibliography of over 700 titles which represent many points of view on the history, culture, and current concerns of Mexican Americans. Includes other cultures.

Catalogs

Bilingual Department, McGraw-Hill.

    Request catalog of bilingual materials. Books in Spanish. Films and books in English as the second language.

Bilingual Educational Services.

    Request catalog of bilingual materials. Includes books, films, filmstrips, prints, posters, games, teacher aids, dictionaries, and multicultural/bilingual sections.

Bilingual Education Service Center.

    Request list of bilingual suppliers. The Materials/Curriculum Specialist offers personal assistance in locating materials.

California State Department of Education.

    Request list of selected publications of the California State Department of Education. Some early childhood publications and inexpensive bilingual publications are available. Limited in cultural resources.

Center for Applied Linguistics.

    Resources and texts for bilingual education including *Handbook of Bilingual Education.*

Chicano Murals. Public Art Workshop.

    Free price list of resources. Several publications on Chicano murals in the Southwest.

Children's Press.

    Bilingual books. Be selective; consider developmental level of children.

Dissemination and Assessment Center for Bilingual Bicultural Education.

    Request list of bilingual-bicultural materials.

E. P. Dutton.

    Spanish editions of popular picture books. Write for their catalog of Windmill Books.

EPIE Report, No. 73: Selector's Guide for Bilingual Education Materials, Vol. 1, Spanish Language Arts, 1975; **EPIE Report, No. 74: Selector's Guide for Bilingual Education Materials, Vol. 2, Spanish "Branch" Programs.** EPIE Institute, 1976.

    Educational Products Information Exchange Institute (EPIE) has compiled two volumes of Spanish instructional materials produced by both commercial and noncommercial companies in the United States and other countries. Each volume includes guidelines for selection of materials and addresses of sources.

Funk and Wagnalls.

    Has published a number of bilingual books written by Alex Rider. Write for a publications list.

Resources for Adults

Institute of Modern Languages.

Publishes materials for teaching a second language to young children. Materials were developed as a total cognitive, affective, and sensorimotor growth program.

National Educational Laboratory Publishers.

Request catalog of bilingual/early childhood filmstrips, records, photographs, and drawings designed to aid in teaching English to Spanish-speaking young children (preschool through grade three). NEL is also the distribution center for ERIC/Clearinghouse on Rural Education and Small Schools.

Office of International and Bilingual Education. Texas Education Agency.

Request publications list.

Penca Books.

Formerly the Cultural Distribution Center. An annotated catalog of over 300 titles on history, literature, and Spanish dictionaries for adults, from more than 200 publishers.

Many publishers have recently added Spanish language books to their lists. Request catalogs from these and other publishers for additional materials. Be sure to check the Spanish for relevance to the Spanish dialect spoken in your community.

Cruzada Spanish Publications.
Iaconi Book Imports.
Las Américas Publishing Co.
Libreria Alma Mater.
Jesús Gonzales Pita.
Spanish Book Corporation of America.

Periodicals

Americas. Organization of American States.

The cultures of the OAS countries are explored through articles about natural resources, literature, history, and folk art. Published monthly in English, Spanish, and Portuguese.

Aztlan-International Journal of Chicano Studies Research. Chicano Studies Center.

A scholarly and academic review of nationally current topics in art and social sciences. Published triannually in English.

Bilingual Review. Department of Foreign Languages.

Contains bilingual information in terms of research, criticism, literature, pedagogy, and bibliographies and reviews.

Cartel. Dissemination and Assessment Center for Bilingual Bicultural Education.

A monthly annotated bibliography of materials for use in bilingual-bicultural education. Informs and supplies criteria for relevance in selecting materials. The cumulative issue (December) may be purchased separately. DACBE, Winter 1975, is an annotated catalog of publications currently available.

La Crónica. Other Options.

Newspaper treatment of Chicano history, 1835 to 1964.

La Luz.

National focus magazine written by and for Spanish Americans. Published monthly in English.

NAVE. Las Americas Publishing Co.

This periodical is the journal of the National Association for Bilingual Education. Subscriptions and/or single copies available.

Northwest Educational Cooperative. Bilingual Education Service Center.

Publishes a monthly newsletter during the school year "to inform readers on bilingual-bicultural issues and activities outside and within the state of Illinois. Persons wishing to receive the newsletter will be added to the mailing list on request."

Revista Chicano-Riqueña. Indiana University Northwest.

A national quarterly bilingual journal of poems, short stories, plays, folklore, and literary criticism by Chicanos and Puerto Ricans.

Sesame Street. Children's Television Workshop.

Bilingual magazine which some children can read. Includes posters, puzzles, and instructions for making instruments and games.

Materials and Experiences

Posters/Pictures

Animales Domésticos. Developmental Learning Materials, 1974.

A color chart of domestic animals labeled in Spanish.

El Calendario Chicano. Southwest Network.

Annual calendar, suitable for adults. Historical events, documented and collected, are listed. Network attempts to place the contemporary Chicano movement in its historical context.

Carteles Puertorriqueños. Distributed by Dissemination and Assessment Center for Bilingual Bicultural Education.

A set of four full-color posters depicting Puerto Ricans past and present, designed to stimulate learning and appreciation of Puerto Rican culture. Subjects: Hombres Ilustres, La Mujer Puertorriqueña, Gobernadores de Puerto Rico, and Mi Raza.

Guias para los Carteles Puertorriqueños. A teacher's resource to be used with the posters. Gives biographical sketches of persons depicted on the posters.

Famous Historical Figures, by Fernandez Editores. Distributed by Bilingual Educational Services.

Color posters of fourteen famous United States Spanish-speaking people.

Mexico, Central America and the West Indies Today: Picture/Story/Study Print. Society for Visual Education.

Color photographs of rural and suburban Mexico: gardens, markets, and festivals. Six sets. Each set contains eight pictures, 18" x 13".

Spanish-Speaking Americans. Enterprises Publications.

Twelve study prints of current newsmaking Spanish-speaking Americans such as Lee Trevino, Vikki Carr, and Anthony Quinn. Spanish-speaking children can identify with all of them. Information in English and Spanish.

Tourist and Travel Offices. Posters and pictures available.
  Aeroméxico—Airline. (Aeronaves de México, South America.)
  Consulates—Check your phone directory.
  Mexican Chamber of Commerce of the United States.
  Mexican Embassy.
  Mexican Government Tourism Department.
  Mexican National Tourist Council.
  Mexicana. (Mexicana de Aviación, South America.)

Records

Bilingual Educational Services.

Resource for José Feliciano records. Set of ten albums includes some favorites.

Canciones Infantiles Mexicanas, by Yolanda del Campo. Produced by Coro. Distributed by Bilingual Educational Services, 1965.

A collection of children's game songs sung by Spanish-speaking children everywhere. These songs can enrich the cultural background knowledge of Spanish-speaking Americans and are especially appropriate for the Southwest.

Cantemos en Español, *Language Through Songs.* Produced by Idyllwild. Distributed by Neil A. Kjos Music Co., 1961.

Recording of Spanish songs for children ages five through eight. Has been used with Spanish- and non-Spanish-speaking children. A teacher's book and a student's book are included with the record.

Cantos de Mexico and **Folksongs of Mexico.** Produced by Idyllwild. Distributed by Neil A. Kjos Music Co., 1968.

Children ages five through eight enjoy the dances and songs. The teacher's guide that is included is a resource for the dances with suggestions for additional activities.

Fray Martin, with Alice Firgau. *Making Music Your Own.* Six-record album. Produced by Silver Burdett. Distributed by General Learning Corporation. Album #75180.

Children learn songs in English and Spanish. They dramatize "tan tan tan tan." Book accompanies album.

Mexican Folk Songs. Produced and distributed by Bowmar.

Popular songs, good technical quality. Some instructions for dances. Words of songs printed on album cover.

Mexican Hand Clapping Chant, with Ella Jenkins. *Little Johnny Brown.* Produced by Folkways Records. Distributed by Scholastic Records. Record #SC7631.

Children enjoy participating in the songs. An enjoyable way to learn Spanish.

Carol Perkins. Produced and distributed by Caper Records.

The seven records are in English and Spanish. Even though the technical production is poor and the pitch of the singing voice too low, children ages five through eight enjoy the songs. Perkins's music is original and has a special appeal to children. Recommended as a resource for teachers.

La Raspa, with Ella Jenkins. *Little Johnny Brown.* Produced by Folkways Records. Distributed by Scholastic Records. Record #SC7631.

An instrumental record of this famous traditional dance. Ella Jenkins is an expert in involving children in movement.

Las Rejas de Chapultepec. Produced by Corito Infantil. Distributed by Bilingual Education Service Center.

A favorite of many teachers. Narrated by Tío Herminio with good enunciation and clarity of expression. Includes stories, games, songs, and poetry.

Spanish-English Basic Awareness, with Lou Stallman and Raoul Gonzales. Distributed by Stallman Educational Systems. Album #TSR2801.

Young children learn Spanish words, phrases, and sentences by singing in English and repeating in Spanish. Includes "Let's Be Friends," "Things in the Room," "Let's Play the Name Game." Children delight in learning to count, learning the names of the days of the week, and learning to use right and left hands for a singing game. Manual included.

A Taste of Education: Building Your Spanish Vocabulary Through Music. Read by Eddie Cano. Distributed by C. P. Records. Record #CP100.

A teacher presents this excellent method of teaching English to Spanish-speaking children and Spanish to children whose first language is English. Children learn vocabulary by repeating Cano's statements.

Materials and Experiences

Films/Filmstrips

Bilingual Early Childhood Program. Audiovisual Approach to Oral Language Development. Scholastic Audio Visual.

Includes teacher's guide and teacher's bilingual reference guide.

Five Families, a cultural awareness sound filmstrip program for early childhood, 1972. Five filmstrips/cassettes.

Includes Black Americans, Navajos, Anglos, Asian Americans, and Mexican Americans, with accompanying music typical of each culture.

Five Children, a cultural awareness sound filmstrip program for early childhood, 1972. Five filmstrips/cassettes.

Includes cowboy, Latin family in New York, fisherman's son, birthday for Howard, and Sara's letter. Information is authentic. Describes the daily life and family activity of American children from different cultural, ethnic, and geographic backgrounds.

Who Am I? ¿Quíen Soy Yo? Series on concept of self, 1970. Five filmstrips/cassettes or phonodisc.

Children of different cultures are depicted in pictures. Topics covered are "joy of being you," "feelings," and "nothing is something to do." Very good for independent use by young children. Highly recommended.

I Can. Four filmstrips/cassettes.

Shows children of all cultures making music in many different ways. Suggests activities for the young child.

The four additional sets of bilingual filmstrips and cassettes in this series deal with beginning concepts and how the child learns. Write to Scholastic Audio Visual for additional information.

Christmas in Mexico/Feliz Navidad. Produced and distributed by Spoken Arts, 1972.

Young children get a glimpse of a Mexican family celebrating Christmas. Children learn about Mexican holiday foods and customs of gift-giving—breaking the piñata and the posada. Teacher's guide is included with filmstrip and cassette.

Cinco Vidas. Produced and distributed by Ruiz Productions.

Life as a Chicano, as revealed through personal portraits of a principal, an attorney, a gardener, a woman who is a representative of Title I projects, and a woman involved in the Mexican-American community as a single elderly person. The film depicts involved persons, from Chicano communities, who are sensitive to the needs of their ethnic group.

Colores en Cuentos, Stories about Color. Produced and distributed by Coronet Films, 1968.

Six filmstrips, six cassettes in Spanish and English: "La Flor Morada (The Purple Flower)," "La Calabaza Anaranjada (The Orange Pumpkin)," "El Pajaro Amarillo (The Yellow Bird)," "El Balón Azul (The Blue Balloon)," "El Carrito Rojo (The Red Car)," "El Gasano Verde (The Green Caterpillar)." For young children through the primary grades. The adventures of several things, of different colors, are presented to help children learn to recognize the colors by name.

Directorio Chicano: A Resource Listing of Chicano Media-Print and Film. Southwest Network, 1976.

Lists films produced by Chicano filmmakers, magazines, newsletters, pino newsletters, journals, research centers, distributors, and publishers. Includes price, frequency, and focus of publication.

Even Yellow Cars Have to Wait in Line. Produced and distributed by Urban Media Materials.

Story of a Puerto Rican family in New York City and in Puerto Rico. About the environment, patience, and taking turns. Filmstrip/cassette in Spanish and English; includes teacher's guide.

Messages in Clay. Produced and distributed by Ruiz Productions.

Film with music accompaniment and brief narration about games, dance, and human relationships dramatized in clay. Excellent for young children.

Mexican Market. Produced and distributed by ACI Films.

Scenes of marketplace near Mexico City give young children a view of a Mexican village. Music of Mexico in background. Available in Spanish or English text; the elementary Spanish text appeals to English-speaking children. ACI films may be rented; request list of rental libraries.

Too, Too, Too Hot. Produced and distributed by Urban Media Materials, 1972.

Story about a child from Santo Domingo who teaches her classmates how the weather helps a palm tree grow. Filmstrip/cassette in English and Spanish, includes teacher's guide.

Villa Alegre. Produced and distributed by Bilingual Children's Television (BC/TV).

Series about Juanito, a six-year-old, as he experiences cultural shock. Objectives are to create an awareness of and respect for other lifestyles and cultural differences and to bring ethnic communities closer together.

Slides

Travel Slides. Produced by Technicolor Corporation. Distributed by Slides Unlimited.

Request a catalog of slides.

Dolls/Games/Flags/Kits

Core, Philip, C. V. Lopez, and L. Peck. **BRL Sullivan for Spanish Speaking Child.** Sullivan's Associates, 1973.

Introduces the child to Spanish reading through a cultural approach. It was developed in Los Angeles but is used across the United States; therefore, standard Spanish is used. Children do not understand all the words, but the introduction of reading through the use of animals results in a high level of interest.

Juan and Juanita Dolls. Childcraft Education Corporation.

Nineteen-inch dolls dressed in fiesta clothes.

Lingo. U.S. Committee for UNICEF. #5001.

A game played like Bingo, using names of nutritious foods in English, French, and Spanish.

Lotería Mexicana: Mexican Bingo. Bilingual Educational Services. #T0810.

Played like Bingo with Mexican handicrafts instead of numbers. Children take turns calling names of the objects from their cards.

Mexican Flags. Bilingual Educational Services.

Authentic Mexican-designed silk flags. 20½" x 36" and 36" x 70".

NELP. National Educational Laboratories Program, Southwest Educational Development Corp., 1973. Distributed by National Educational Laboratory Publishers.

A bicultural-bilingual program, developed in McAllen, Texas, for kindergarten and primary grade children. The kindergarten kit contains records with traditional Mexican folksongs sung by Mexican Americans. It also includes dance

Materials and Experiences

steps to be performed to the music. The Spanish is that of the Texas Mexican American, and all visual materials include Mexican Americans.

BOLAK (Bilingual Oral Language and Reading Program) — The first and second grade readers are also written in the vernacular of the Mexican-American child and include stories familiar to that culture.

Museums

Locate museums in your community that may be appropriate for children.

Pete Kitchen Western Museum.

The museum is located on the oldest ranch in Arizona. It contains Spanish furniture and armor dating from the days of the conquistadors, Spanish colonial weapons, and original paintings from Spanish missions.

Old Mission San Luis Rey.

Displays Mexican artifacts, Indian artifacts, manuscripts, Spanish paintings, statues, and other objects in the old mission built by Luiseno Indians in 1798 and restored in 1892.

San Jacinto Museum of History Association.

Artifacts on Texan, Mexican, and regional history are displayed in the base of the San Jacinto monument. Includes paintings, engravings, pictures, coins, and costumes illustrating Spanish-Mexican influences on the development of Texas culture.

San Juan Bautista State Historic Park.

A preservation project featuring buildings of the Mission, Mexican, and California Early American periods. Includes the Spanish Soldiers' Barracks, Plaza Hotel, Castro Adobe, and Plaza Stable. The buildings contain authentic furnishings and relics of the times, including a collection of vehicles.

Tumacacori National Monument.

Features a museum collection on Spanish mission history in the Southwest United States and Northwest Mexico. Historic buildings. Includes a library on Spanish colonial exploration and the history of Arizona and Mexico.

Festivals/Fairs/Celebrations

The following are a few popular festivals; locate celebrations in your area.

Days in Spain Fiesta. St. Augustine, Florida, Chamber of Commerce.

A colorful fiesta commemorates the city's founding in 1565. Spanish handicrafts and foods are sold and residents dress in Spanish attire. Held annually in mid-August.

Desert Festival. Borrego Springs, California, Chamber of Commerce.

Commemorates the state's Mexican and Spanish heritage. The celebration of the "Days of the Dons" includes a parade, dance performances, strolling mariachi players, a crafts and art show, and campfire programs.

La Fiesta de San Lorenzo. Bernalillo, New Mexico, Albuquerque Chamber of Commerce.

Features Los Matchines dances brought to the New World by Spanish missionaries and colonists. Los Abuelos (the clowns) provide comic relief. Festivities begin with a commemoration of the arrival of the Coronado expedition in 1540. Indians from several pueblos present ceremonial dances. Held annually in mid-August.

Latin-American Fiesta. Mission District, San Francisco, California, San Francisco Convention and Visitors Bureau.

A parade with floats, drill corps, mounted units, bands, and novelty entries. A coronation ball features Latin-American musicians and dancers. Sponsored by the Spanish-Speaking Citizens Foundation. Held annually in early May.

Mexican-American Festival. Scottsbluff, Nebraska, Chamber of Commerce.

Descendants of original Mexican settlers celebrate their heritage. Features a fine display of Mexican folk dancing and a large exhibit of ornate and beautiful Mexican crafts. Held annually in mid-September.

San Luis Rey Fiesta and Barbecue. Mission San Luis Rey, Oceanside, California, San Diego Convention and Visitors Bureau.

Mexican and Spanish dancers, musicians, and actors provide continuous entertainment. Visitors participate in games, rides, and street dancing. Los Caballeros del Camino Real, one hundred trek riders in authentic costume, arrive after an overnight campout for a traditional ceremony. Held annually in late July.

Tucson Festival. Tucson, Arizona, Festival Society.

Salutes the multicultural heritage of the city, founded as a fortified Spanish settlement in 1775. Includes a month-long series of festivals with Spanish, Mexican, Indian, and pioneer themes. Held annually in April.

* * *

Acknowledgements

Appreciation for assistance in preparing the Spanish-Speaking Americans chapter is expressed to: Elva Allie, bilingual kindergarten teacher in the Fort Worth Independent School District, and a graduate student at North Texas State University; and Odalmira L. Garcia, assistant in the bilingual program, Southwest Educational Development Laboratory, Austin, Texas, and a doctoral student in early childhood education at the University of Texas.

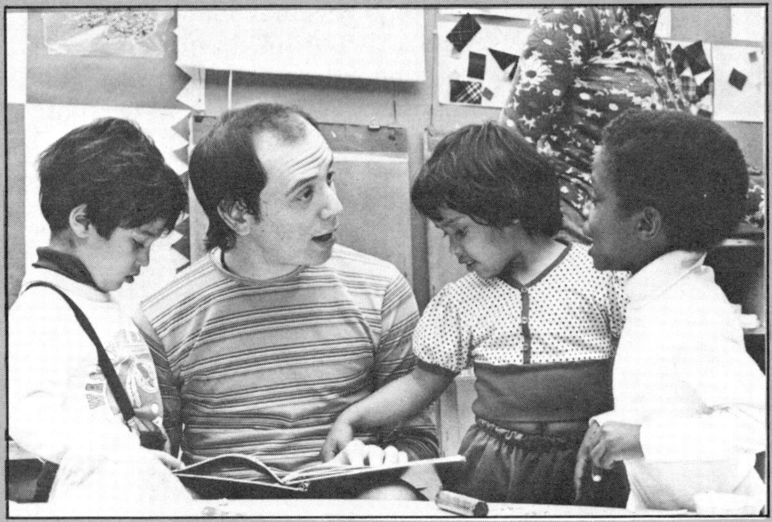

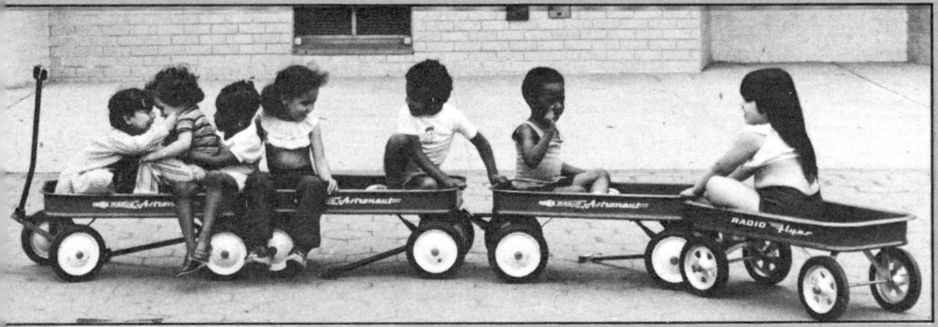
Astronaut
RADIO

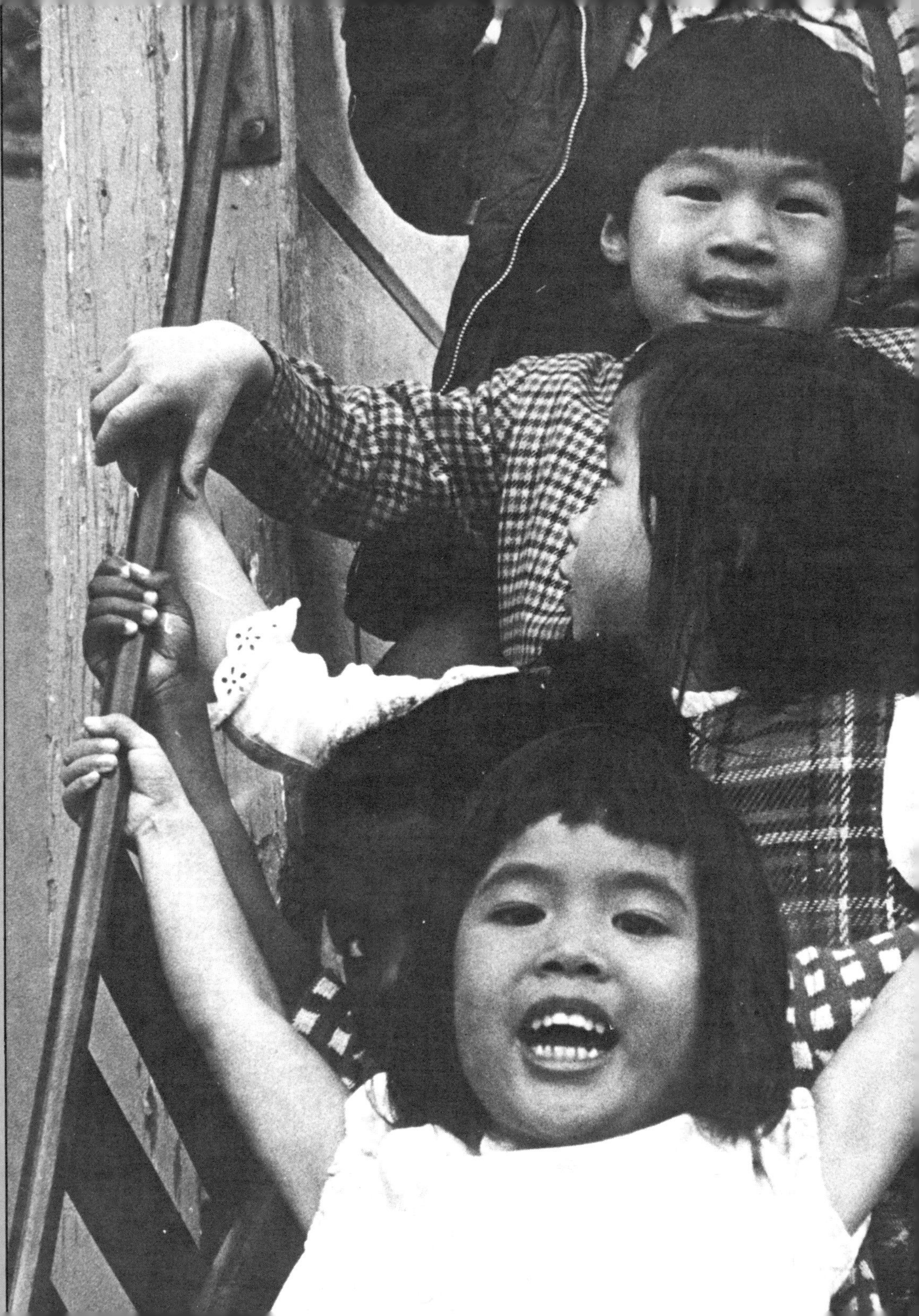

Multicultural Resources

Books for Children

About Us: The Childcraft Annual. Field Enterprises Educational Corporation, 1973. NK

> Explores cultures of "the people of the planet Earth." Photographs are authentic and artistic.

Adoff, Arnold. **Black Is Brown Is Tan.** Harper & Row, 1973. NKP

> An experience in integration. Well done; fills the void of books that project positive relationships between cultural groups.

Baer, Edith. **The Wonder of Hands.** Parents' Magazine Press, 1970. NK

> Hands can do all kinds of things. Photographs of Black and White faces and hands are portrayed effectively.

Baron, Virginia Olsen, ed. **Here I Am! An Anthology of Poems Written by Young People in Some of America's Minority Groups.** Dutton, 1969. KP

> Blacks, Eskimos, and Navajos are among the contributors of these sensitive, insightful poems. "Hunting Whale" by Sally Nashookpuk and "My Home" by Jones Saltwater are special for children.

Bond, Jean Carey. **Brown Is a Beautiful Color.** Watts, 1969. KP

> Pleasures of the color brown are exclaimed by a young child in poetic form with full-page illustrations by Barbara Zuber. Positive association of color is initiated by these two Black artists.

Buffet, Guy, and P. Buffet. **Adventures of Kama Pua'a.** Island Heritage, 1972. KP

> Full-page watercolor paintings and a text with Hawaiian names and words retell a story about a boar with magic powers born to a human family. Drama potential. This Hawaiian folktale provides an exceptional language adventure for young children.

Buffet, Guy, and P. Buffet. **Pua Pua Lena Lena and the Magic Kihapu.** Island Heritage, 1972. KP

> Chiefess Lu'ukia and the people of Waipi'o are unhappy. Full-page bold watercolor illustrations and brief text, saturated with Hawaiian words, present an adventure about a thirty-foot spotted dog and how he brings peace to the valley.

Children of Dallas. **Look at Me!** Dallas Public Library, 1973. NK

> Experiences of children of Dallas, told by themselves. Insightful book with authentic photos and brief essays about families, neighborhoods, and "me"—all cultures.

Cooper, Terry Touff. **Many Hands Cooking: An International Cookbook for Girls and Boys.** UNICEF. Crowell, 1972. NKP

> Recipes from many lands.

Frasconi, Antonio. **See and Say.** Harcourt Brace Jovanovich, 1955. KP

   A picture book in four languages—French, Italian, Spanish, and English. Each language is printed in a different color. Useful for learning words from different languages. Illustrated by Frasconi's famous woodcuts.

Glubok, Shirley. **Dolls Dolls Dolls.** Follett, 1975. KPA

   Photographs of dolls in museums include an Eskimo, a Sioux, a Navajo man and woman, an Ashanti flat doll carried by women and girls as a religious object. Children learn about cultures by exploring photographs. Adult text.

Hautzig, Esther. **At Home: A Visit in Four Languages.** Illustrated by Aliki. Macmillan, 1969. KP

   In School: Learning in Four Languages. Illustrated by Nonny Hogrogian. Macmillan, 1969. KP

   In the Park: An Excursion in Four Languages. Illustrated by Ezra Jack Keats. Macmillan, 1969. KP

   This set of books teaches the words for objects in Spanish, English, Russian, and French. Each book is illustrated by a well-known artist.

Heide, Florence Parry. **My Castle.** McGraw-Hill, 1972. NK

   Young minority child reacts in a creative, imaginative way to his multiethnic neighborhood and to special visitors who intrude into the "castle" and physical surroundings of the fire escape. Symbolic nature of the story adds dimension. The cozy, comfortable, supportive illusion the fire escape castle gives is illustrated by Symeon Shimin in watercolor and pencil sketches. A beautiful, rare literary experience.

Joseph, Joan. **Folk Toys Around the World and How to Make Them.** Parents' Magazine Press, 1972. KP

   Most of the toys present a challenge for young children. Adaptations can be made, and children are the first to discover other ways to make things.

Lester, Julius. **Who I Am.** Dial, 1974. KP

   Multiethnic experiences in photographs by David Gahrs and poems by Lester. Be selective with young children.

Mangurain, David. **Lito the Shoeshine Boy.** Four Winds, 1975. KP

   Daily life of young boy in Honduras enables children to view a culture that is economically depressed but allows good feelings and responsibility to flourish.

Merrill, Jean, and F. G. Seset. **How Many Kids Are Hiding on My Block?** Whitman, 1973. NK

   Rico, Igor, Su Lu, Carlotta, and other neighborhood friends play Hide and Seek. Clever demonstration of integration.

Pine, Tillie S., and J. Levine. **The Polynesians Knew.** McGraw-Hill, 1974. KP

   Instructions for making instruments, carving, keeping records, building huts, printing designs, and making baskets are included. Historical sketches.

Poignant, Axel. **Bush Walkabout.** Addison-Wesley, 1972. KP

   Rikili and Nullagundi, Aborigine children, explore the rain forest of northern Australia. Full-page photographs and descriptive text give the reader a cultural view. Trapping a goanna, securing water from a tree, camping out in a paper bark tent, and having a corroboree to celebrate are of interest to young children.

Poignant, Axel, and R. Poignant. **Kaleku.** Addison-Wesley, 1975. KP

   A geography experience through superb color and black and white photographs, with a narrative for older children. Young children inquire about interesting happenings—wedding festivities, pig chase, market visit, storytelling with grandfather, and a nostalgic glance at his home as Kaleku leaves for school in Kundiawa, "far away over the mountains." The importance of combining old and new ways in

New Guinea is voiced in this beautiful book. However, there is an offensive portrayal of a girl who whines while a boy is brave.

Raposo, Joe. **Being Green.** Western Publishing, 1973. NK

"It's not that easy being green." Deals with positive and negative facets of being any particular color. Acceptance of own color is the theme.

Raynor, Dorka. **Grandparents Around the World.** Whitman, 1977. KP

Photos of children and their grandparents from twenty-five countries depict much about their lives.

Raynor, Dorka. **This Is My Father and Me.** Whitman, 1973. NK

Photographic collection with brief description explores the cultural aspect of fathers and their children. One of the few photo books that provide authentic situations and realistically reflect relationships. Young children can view photographs of families from numerous countries.

Sargent, Jessie F. **Kids of Colómbia.** Addison-Wesley, 1974. NK

Huge, magnificent country inhabited by charming young children is described with black and white photographs. Effort is made by the author and the photographer, Ulrike Welsch, to interest young children in different cultures "in the hopes that children, who once were strangers because the world was so big, will not remain isolated through fear of each other."

Simon, Norma. **All Kinds of Families.** Whitman, 1976. NK

Acknowledges that families are not always composed in the traditional way. Young children need books that reflect numerous patterns of family behavior. The "patchwork quilt family" symbolizes a celebration of diversity, beauty, responsiveness, and stability.

Simon, Norma. **I Know What I Like.** Whitman, 1971. NK

Significant because of the attempt to positively project integrated communities. Simon is "especially aware of the need for books that deal realistically with everyday life." Grandmother may be stereotyped.

Simon, Norma. **What Do I Say?** Whitman, 1973. NK

Manuel, a Puerto Rican child, has a Black teacher and White and Black friends. Also available in Spanish/English edition.

Temko, Florence. **Folk Crafts for World Friendship.** Doubleday, 1976. KP

Masks, costumes, celebrations, toys, decorations, and games from numerous cultures. A history of the traditional crafts with step-by-step directions.

Zim, Jacob, ed. **My Shalom My Peace: Paintings and Poems by Jewish and Arab Children.** McGraw-Hill, 1974. KP

Peace is the theme of this beautiful book illustrated with numerous line drawings and halftones. The insight and profundity of the poems are moving. Collection was taken from school children in Israel who have slept in shelters, witnessed wars, and known death.

Resources for Adults

Books and Articles

Children and Intercultural Education. Association for Childhood Education International, 1974.

Three minibulletins: "Some Minorities Speak Out," "Overview and Research," and "Are There Unwelcome Guests in Your Classroom?" A large number of cultures in America are included. Many practical suggestions for adults who work with minority children. Covers all aspects of education.

Cohen, Monroe D., ed. **Neighbors.** Association for Childhood Education International, 1972.

A collection of articles from *Childhood Education* on multicultural education.

Cohen, Robert. **The Color of Man.** Random House, 1968.

Large photographs by Ken Heyman complement the text researched by experts in the fields of biology, anthropology, sociology, and psychology. Adult text gives scientific data. Young children can browse through the full-page black and white photographs to experience the beauty of life displayed by people of numerous cultures.

Coles, Robert. **Teachers and the Children of Poverty.** Potomac Institute, 1970.

Robert Coles, a psychiatrist, wrote this book based on a study of the transactions between students and teachers. He describes and analyzes the successes and failures of education by what is happening to children. Valuable for the teacher who wants to improve effectiveness with children of many cultures.

Corcoran, Gertrude B. **Language Experiences for Nursery and Kindergarten Years.** Peacock, 1976.

Background beliefs about how young children learn language; includes activities to develop language. The chapter on using literature, music, and art to develop language and the list of books for children in the appendix are valuable.

Ethnic Chronology Series: Chronology and Fact Books. Oceana, 1971.

Sixteen volumes concerning sixteen ethnic groups. The basic format of each volume is a chronological section of significant events supported by a documentary section, a selected bibliography, and special features related to the particular group.

Ethnic Heritage Studies Program. Indiana University at South Bend.

This program is funded to identify, adapt, and disseminate culturally pluralistic curriculum materials for the following ethnic groups: African, Hungarian, Italian, Mexican, and Polish Americans.

Resources for Adults

Gold, Milton J., C. A. Grant, and H. N. Rivlin, eds. **In Praise of Diversity: A Resource Book for Multicultural Education.** Association of Teacher Educators, 1977.

Volume on America's pluralism for educational personnel, both those inservice and those preparing to teach. Stresses positive values of difference, diversity, and pluralism.

Gonzalez-Mena, Janet. **English as a Second Language for Preschool Children.** *Young Children* 32, no. 1 (November 1976): 14-19. National Association for the Education of Young Children.

Principles for establishing a second language program for young children. Emphasizes that "children learn language best in real situations with concrete experiences."

Gordon, Milton M., ed. **Ethnic Groups in American Life Series.** Prentice-Hall, 1971.

Eight titles covering brief history of many ethnic groups, including Black Americans, Indian Americans, Japanese Americans, Mexican Americans, and Puerto Rican Americans. Volumes include bibliographies.

Grant, Gloria W. **Criteria Cultural Pluralism in the Classroom.** *Educational Leadership* 32 (December 1974): 190-192.

Lists seventeen elements of a culturally pluralistic curriculum. Helpful to teachers in understanding the influence the curriculum has on the attitudes of students. Suggests how to prepare the environment for this situation.

Grant, Gloria W., ed. **In Praise of Diversity: Multicultural Classroom Applications.** Center for Urban Education, 1977.

Discusses activities for the classroom teacher interested in implementing multicultural education. Subject areas include social studies, language arts, science/math, and art.

Human Relations Workshop. Southern Methodist University/National Conference of Christians and Jews (NCCJ).

The workshop examines causes of tensions and problems among different groups in American society. Examines prejudice and evaluates solutions for intergroup problems. Special emphasis is placed on multicultural education. Scholarships offered from NCCJ. Check with colleges in your community for similar workshops.

Johnson, Harry A. **Guide to Media and Materials on Ethnic American Minorities.** Bowker, 1975.

A reference book from a publisher that specializes in reference sources. Available in most libraries.

Kositsky, Val. **What in the World Is Cooking in Class Today? Multiethnic Recipes for Young Children.** *Young Children* 33, no. 1 (November 1977): 23-31. National Association for the Education of Young Children.

Recipes for cooking in the classroom gathered from a number of cultural groups.

Lane, Mary B. **Education for Parenting.** National Association for the Education of Young Children, 1975.

Experiences with families in the Cross-Cultural Family Center in San Francisco.

Lane, Mary B., and others. **Nurseries in Cross-Cultural Education.** San Francisco State College, 1971.

Final report of an experimental five-year program in San Francisco. The project studied the processes of involving inner-city families of various cultures in coping with problems. An interaction model was developed that could be utilized with groups of people anywhere. This was one of the more successful experiments combining education of young children with helping families.

Mead, Margaret. **People and Places.** Bantam, 1970.

Study of cultures, with special emphasis on Eskimos, Indians of the Plains, Ashanti, Balinese, and Minoans.

Miller, Carl S. **Sing Children Sing: Songs, Dances and Singing Games of Many Lands and Peoples.** Chappell, 1972. Distributed by Quadrangle/New York Times.

The basic fabric of patterns and series is universal, substantiated by this book of songs of different ethnic groups. Children easily learn these tunes from numerous cultures. Photographs on each page add meaning for young children.

Montebello, Mary S. **Children's Literature in the Curriculum.** Brown, 1972.

Good reviews; criteria for selecting books.

Moquin, Wayne, ed. **Makers of America.** 10 vols. Encyclopaedia Britannica Educational Corporation, 1971.

Brief history from 1536 to 1970. The editor has made an effort to include the role and contributions of minorities in each volume.

The National Children's Directory. Urban Information Interpreters. 1977.

Lists local, state, and national organizations active in the area of children's rights and welfare. It includes groups seeking to bring about change in such areas as children's media, day care, public schools, and legal rights of children.

Pialorsi, Frank, ed. **Teaching the Bilingual.** University of Arizona Press, 1974.

How to integrate new methods with old traditions in Spanish-speaking, Black, and Navajo cultures. Also treats the psychological effects of bilingualism.

Sciara, Frank J., and L. W. Dunworth. **Helps for Teaching in the Integrated Classroom.** Economics Press, 1971.

A booklet of twenty pointers for evaluating yourself as the teacher of a multicultural classroom, with suggestions for improving your rating.

Spicer, Dorothy G. **The Book of Festivals.** Gale Research Co., 1969.

Study by folklorist presents folk customs of many peoples "to show that festivals are but one of many forces that unite nations and give continuity to cultural thought."

Stauffer, Russell G. **The Language-Experience Approach to the Teaching of Reading.** Harper & Row, 1970.

The first three chapters help adults in using the child's language in prereading activities. This method shows respect for the child's home language; the approach can be used with any language.

Stereotypes, Distortions and Omissions in U.S. History Textbooks. Council on Interracial Books for Children, 1976.

This book is a content analysis instrument for detecting racism and sexism. It combines informative chapters with detailed charts against which you can readily check your own textbooks' treatment of African, Asian, Mexican, and Native Americans; Puerto Ricans; and women. Reference sources document each item, comprising an extensive and valuable annotated bibliography.

U.S. Commission on Civil Rights. **Better Chance to Learn: Bilingual-Bicultural Education.** U.S. Government Printing Office, Superintendent of Documents, 1975.

The purpose of this bulletin is to explain bilingual-bicultural education and suggest ways of equalizing educational opportunity for bilingual children. Topics included are self-concept, cognitive and language development, culture and learning, and research resources. Publication No. 51, Item 288-A.

von Maltitz, Frances W. **Living and Learning in Two Languages.** McGraw-Hill, 1975.

Gives rationale, programs, and practices about bilingual-bicultural education in the United States. Includes Native American, Asian American, and Spanish-speaking cultures.

Resources for Adults

Valuable sections on sources of information and materials and on how other countries approach bilingual education.

Wasserman, Paul J., and J. Morgan, eds. **Ethnic Information Sources of the United States.** Gale Research Co., 1976.

A guide to organizations, agencies, foundations, institutions, media, commercial and trade bodies, government programs, research institutes, libraries and museums, religious organizations, banking firms, festivals and fairs, travel and tourist offices, airlines and ship lines, book dealers and publishers' representatives, and books, pamphlets, and audiovisuals on specific ethnic groups. Includes numerous minorities, but excludes Blacks, Native Americans, and Eskimos!

Wasserman, Paul J., and others, eds. **Festivals Sourcebook.** Gale Research Co., 1977.

A reference guide to fairs, festivals, and celebrations in agriculture, antiques, the arts, theater and drama, arts and crafts, community, dance, ethnic events, film, folk, food and drink, history, Indians, marine life, music, seasons, and wildlife. Resource of more than 3,800 festivals, fairs, and community celebrations in the United States and Canada. Helpful aid for planning interest trips and providing contacts for further information.

Wynar, Lubomyr R. **Encyclopedic Directory of Ethnic Organizations in the United States.** Libraries Unlimited, 1975.

Listing of organizations that assist minority cultures.

Zintz, Miles V. **Education Across Cultures.** Kendall/Hunt, 1969.

The author addresses the problems of educating across cultures in the Southwest. Includes many practical suggestions for teachers as well as information to help them understand various lifestyles. Zintz is authoritative in this field. The book is valuable, even though it is dated.

Bibliographies

Carlson, Ruth K. **Emerging Humanity: Multi-Ethnic Literature for Children and Adolescents.** Brown, 1973.

Discusses types of ethnic literature. Includes chapters on Black Americans, linked with their African heritage; Native American heritage of folktale and song and conflicts of the struggles of Native Americans today; and Mexican Americans' rich cultural heritage and problems today. Each section has a bibliography that includes primary through adolescent level books and professional books.

Cashman, Marc, ed. **Bibliography of American Ethnology.** Bicentennial 1st ed. Todd, 1976.

The 4,500 books listed on ethnology and race relations are divided into four main categories: general ethnology, American Indians, Black Americans, and other minority groups. Most of the entires are annotated. Some of the subcategories are arts and crafts, children, culture and customs, dance, education, folklore, health care, language, leaders, literature, music, and poetry.

Cohen, David, coor. **Multi-Ethnic Media.** American Library Association, Task Force on Ethnic Materials Information Exchange, Office for Library Service to the Disadvantaged, 1975.

Annotated selected bibliographies about minorities, especially about how current textbooks and literature treat minorities.

Educational Resources Information Center (ERIC) Clearinghouses.

All of the sixteen clearinghouses acquire, review, abstract, and index the documents announced in Resources in Education, a monthly publication. The clearinghouses also prepare bibliographies and interpretive summaries of research that appear in the journal and are disseminated through the ERIC Document Reproduction Service.

    ERIC Clearinghouse on Career Education
    ERIC Clearinghouse on Counseling and Personnel Services
    ERIC Clearinghouse on Early Childhood Education
    ERIC Clearinghouse on Educational Management
    ERIC Clearinghouse on Handicapped and Gifted Children
    ERIC Clearinghouse on Higher Education
    ERIC Clearinghouse on Information Resources
    ERIC Clearinghouse on Junior Colleges
    ERIC Clearinghouse on Languages and Linguistics
    ERIC Clearinghouse on Reading and Communication Skills
    ERIC Clearinghouse on Rural Education and Small Schools
    ERIC Clearinghouse on Science, Mathematics, and Environmental Education
    ERIC Clearinghouse on Social Studies/Social Science Education
    ERIC Clearinghouse on Teacher Education
    ERIC Clearinghouse on Tests, Measurement, and Evaluation
    ERIC Clearinghouse on Urban Education

Giese, James. **Multicultural Education: A Functional Bibliography for Teachers.** Center for Urban Education, 1977.

Prepared to accompany *In Praise of Diversity: A Resource Book for Multicultural Education* (see page 94), this book includes multicultural listings and references on prejudice and discrimination. Materials for use at elementary, secondary, and adult levels.

Human (and Anti-Human) Values in Children's Books. Council on Interracial Books for Children, annual edition.

Guidelines for parents, educators, and librarians. Books are examined for sexism, racism, materialism, elitism, individualism, conformism, escapism, and ageism—as well as for cultural authenticity and effect on the self-image of female and/or minority children. A "Values Rating Checklist" shows how each book scores.

Maehr, Jane. **The Middle East: An Annotated Bibliography of Literature for Children.** Educational Resources Information Center on Early Childhood Education (ERIC/ECE), 1977.

Lists more than 400 books for children about ten Middle East countries.

Miller, Wayne C., and others, eds. **A Comprehensive Bibliography for the Study of American Minorities.** Vols. I and II. New York University Press, 1976.

These two volumes contain 29,300 annotated English language entries about more than forty minorities representing every continent. Bibliographies, periodicals, history, biography, the arts, and other subjects are covered. Materials are for adults.

Minority Affairs Multi-Ethnic Handbook. Vols. 2 and 3. Michigan Education Association.

Annotated bibliographies of material concerning racism, Blacks, Chicanos, and Native Americans. Includes films, filmstrips, and literature for various age levels.

Multicultural Aspects of American Life and Education: An Annotated Bibliography. Multilingual Assessment Program, New York Component, 1976. Distributed by Dissemination and Assessment Center for Bilingual Bicultural Education.

Resource book with extensive information on current developments in bilingual education. Includes information on the historical, economic, sociological, and anthropological aspects of Puerto Ricans, Mexican Americans, Cubans, Blacks, Native Americans, and other groups in the United States. Emphasis is on testing, cognitive styles, and teacher training. In English.

Nance, Elizabeth. **A Community of People: A Multi-Ethnic Bibliography.** Portland Public Schools, Educational Media Department, 1974.

One of the most informative annotated bibliographies available. Includes sections for African, Asian, Jewish, Mexican, Native, Puerto Rican, and multiracial Americans.

Nichols, Margaret S., and P. O'Neill. **Multicultural Materials: A Selected Bibliography.** Multicultural Resources, 1974.

Adult materials concerning Black, Chicano, Asian American, and Native American cultures in areas of human relations, history, culture, and current social issues.

Nichols, Margaret S., and P. O'Neill. **Multicultural Resources for Children.** Multicultural Resources, 1977.

A bibliography of materials in the areas of Black, Spanish-speaking, Asian American, Native American, and Pacific Island cultures. For children from preschool through elementary school.

Nichols, Margaret S., and P. O'Neill. **Multi-Ethnic Reading and AV Materials for Young Children: Annotated Bibliography.** Day Care and Child Development Council of America, 1972. Distributed by Gryphon House.

Brief listing of multiethnic materials.

Oaks, Priscilla. **Minority Studies: A Selected Annotated Bibliography.** Hall, 1975.

Entries on Native, Spanish-speaking, African, and Asian Americans. Categories within each culture include bibliographies, periodicals, education, general culture, literature of and about that culture, and arts and crafts.

Root, Shelton L., Jr., and National Council of Teachers of English. **Adventuring with Books.** Citation, 1973.

Over 2,400 titles for prekindergarten through grade eight. Two sections are especially helpful: "Other Lands and People" and "Folk Literature."

Selected Bibliographic Materials on Multiethnic Media. American Library Association.

This is an annotated thirty-three-page bibliography on material about Black, Spanish-speaking, and Native Americans. Also includes some works on Jewish, Italian, Greek, and Polish Americans.

Stokes, Evelyn, and C. D. Henderson. **Ethnic Studies: Black, Indian, Mexican American.** Texas Department of Community Affairs, Early Childhood Development Division, 1975.

Importance of booklet is in its bibliography. Emphasizes competencies, objectives, evaluation, and learning encounters.

Words Like Freedom. California Association of School Librarians.

An annotated bibliography of over 700 titles that represent many points of view on the history, culture, and current concerns of Asian, Black, Mexican, and Native Americans.

Catalogs

Aardvark Media.

Bilingual-bicultural catalog lists new materials in Spanish and English. New supplementary reading series emphasizes materials with children from various ethnic backgrounds.

Addison-Wesley Publishing Co.

Request list of ethnic books. Address request to the attention of the Promotion Department, Children's Books.

Anti-Defamation League of B'nai B'rith.

Publishes print and nonprint materials on many cultures. Examples: *Little Stories*, by G. B. Bond, about children of various racial, religious, and ethnic backgrounds; *Guidelines for Testing Minority Group Children*; and *Books for Friendships*, an annotated list of books recommended for children. Address requests to Book Department.

Multicultural Resources

Baker & Taylor.

Baker & Taylor publishes numerous catalogs, including cultural materials:

Guide to High Interest/Easy Comprehension Multi Media Materials. Brief catalog of ethnic titles.

Paperback Selection Guide. Lists folktales and ethnic fiction for children from kindergarten through grade eight.

Elementary Schools Selection Guide—Supplement. Contains list of ethnic books and audiovisual materials in early childhood and Spanish language materials.

Bilingual Resource Centers.

Title VII resource centers provide assistance in program planning, administration, and evaluation of bilingual/bicultural education, and staff training.

Regional Cross-Cultural Training and Resource Center.

The Multilingual Multicultural Resource and Training Center of New England.

BABEL Resource Center. Bilingual materials.

The National Assessment and Dissemination Center for Bilingual/Bicultural Education. Has Spanish, Portuguese, Oriental, Native American, Greek, Italian, and French materials. Write for list of materials, specifying language.

Bowmar.

Request list of multicultural materials. Catalog includes the following sections: "Folk Songs of Africa," "Favorite Songs of Japanese Children," "North American Indian Songs," "Children's Songs of Mexico," "Music of the Black Man in America," and numerous others.

Childcraft Education Corporation.

Numerous ethnic materials include books, records, instruments.

Children's Books and Recordings. New York Public Library.

Many ethnic books included, categorized by subject. Select the ones suitable for young children.

Children's Press.

Order catalog of adult and children's resources. Select from Raintree Editions: *I'd Rather Stay Home, Doing Things Together, Primary Books for Bilingual Education,* and *Enchantment of Africa* series.

Constructive Playthings.

Request catalog of early childhood and special education materials. Descriptive lists of ethnic materials include books, films, records, dolls.

Day Care and Child Development Council of America.

"Resources for Child Care," a publications catalog, lists African, Asian, and Puerto Rican American themes. Reviews books that best reflect realities and needs of a multicultural society.

Dial Press/Delacorte Press.

Request "Books for Schools and Libraries" catalog. A graded catalog with curriculum-related index.

The Dissemination and Assessment Center for Bilingual/Bicultural Education.

Has Spanish, Navajo, Portuguese, and French materials. Request list of materials, specifying language.

Encyclopaedia Britannica Educational Corporation.

Request filmstrip, film, book, study prints, recording, and transparencies catalog. Lists American Indian legends (some stereotyped illustrations) and American folktales.

Focus on Minorities: A Multicultural Booklist for Children in the Primary and Intermediate Grades. Crowell.

This catalog has a professional tone with annotations and a key to recommendations by basic selection tools. Included are books dealing with the Black experience, American Indians,

Resources for Adults

Spanish-speaking children, and Oriental Americans. Also includes books with a multiethnic focus. The publisher has been especially active in the publication of books for minority children.

Follett Publishing Co.

Will send catalog on request. Includes list of suggested titles that focus on ethnic materials.

Four Winds Press/Scholastic Press.

Order catalog with recommended ethnic books for young readers. "Starline Books" catalog also lists ethnic reading resources.

Harcourt Brace Jovanovich.

Annotated list by title, subject, and author of available materials. Publishes bilingual books written by Antonio Frasconi. Request publications catalog.

Information Center on Children's Cultures. U.S. Committee for UNICEF.

Collection of educational and cultural materials for kindergarten through grade four. Includes booklists, information sheets, and teaching units. Suggestions for related resources—films, recordings, pictures, photographs, children's art, games, and musical instruments.

Institute of Texas Cultures.

Publishes a monthly bulletin with information about persons from diverse cultures who settled Texas and have contributed to progress in the state. Booklets are available on each of these cultures. Request list of publications. Institute has a multimedia presentation, exhibits, and a multicultural folk festival in August each year.

Macmillan Library Services.

Request catalog for elementary school libraries, which includes filmstrips and books. Subject collections with descriptive references. Films on African legends and folktales included.

Miller-Brody Productions.

"Motivations Book/Related Programs" catalog. Direct attention to cultural awareness, folktales of ethnic America for young readers, and bilingual sections.

Monthly Catalog of United States Government Publications. U.S. Government Printing Office, Superintendent of Documents.

Annotated listing of new government bulletins on all subjects, including cultural awareness and young children. Some bulletins are bilingual. Annual cumulative issue also published. Catalogs are available in most public and school libraries.

National Council of Teachers of English.

Request "Resources for English and Language Arts/Catalog of Publications." Annotated bibliography includes "Haiku in English," "Criteria for Teaching Materials in Reading and Literature," "Task Force on Racism and Bias in the Teaching of English," and "Literature by and about the American Indian." Numerous booklists on dialects.

Noble and Noble, Publishers.

Instructional materials catalog. Numerous resources useful for African studies.

Office of Multi-Ethnic Series. McGraw-Hill.

Resources for adults and young children in "Multiethnic Materials" catalog. Includes audiovisual materials.

Parnassus Press.

"Books for Young People" lists numerous multicultural materials.

Public Documents.

Request catalog of multiethnic publications. Children's books, kindergarten through junior high school. Descriptive list of books dealing with ethnic studies.

Selected U.S. Government Publications. U.S. Government Printing Office, Superintendent of Documents.

Lists new publications. Materials also relate to multiethnic studies. Bimonthly. Request that your name be placed on their mailing list.

R. H. Stone.

Request "Selection Book for Your Style of Teaching" catalog; see multiethnic materials.

Viking Press.

Order "Viking Junior Books" catalog. Annotated list, categorized in graded subject index.

Albert Whitman and Co.

Request catalog "Books for Girls and Boys." See index for urban/ethnic section.

Periodicals

The American Folklore Newsletter. American Folklore Society (AFS).

Published quarterly and distributed to AFS members. Newsletter available on request. Notes job openings in ethnic studies and lists publication of books, records, and films.

Bulletin of Human Values in Children's Literature. Council on Interracial Books for Children.

Reviews new children's books about various countries and American minorities. Subscription includes eight bulletins per year.

Bulletin of the Council on Interracial Books for Children. Council on Interracial Books for Children.

Promotes antiracist and antisexist literature as well as instructional materials for children. The council has established a yearly contest for unpublished minority writers of children's literature. Also conducts clinics and provides resource specialists in awareness training sessions. Honest and forthright reviews of children's books. Request subscription information; back issues are available and inexpensive. The bilingual-bicultural packet of twelve items is #C-4.

Crowell Book News. Crowell.

Interesting information about new books, many of them ethnic in nature. Published quarterly. Free posters offered.

ERIC/ECE Newsletter. Educational Resources Information Center Clearinghouse on Early Childhood Education.

A valuable resource. Selected references from ERIC in early childhood education with several feature articles. Bibliographies, new books, and other resources with ordering information are included in each issue. Includes bilingual-bicultural-multicultural early childhood resources. Four issues per year.

National Geographic World. National Geographic Society.

A magazine for children, with pictures of many cultures. Reading level is fifth grade and up. The adult magazine, *National Geographic*, is a rich resource for adults on all cultures and includes authentic photographs.

Time/Out. Creative Communications.

A new bimonthly children's magazine. Along with poems, puzzles, and stories, the Spring 1976 issue includes answers to questions about minorities. For children in grades two through six.

The Workbook.

Monthly source of information about environmental, social, and consumer problems. Includes minority concerns.

Materials and Experiences

Posters

About Myself. Bowmar, 1968.

Three sets of colorful, large, multiethnic study prints showing children doing a variety of things that pertain to the concept of self and family atmosphere. Titles are "Other People Around Me," "My Family—My Home," and "Myself."

Festival Figures. U.S. Committee for UNICEF, 1971-72.

Three sets of large cut-out figures of people from Latin America, the Caribbean Region, and the Mediterranean and Around the World. Eight figures in each set.

Living Together in America. Cook, 1973.

Titles and manual for adults are in Spanish and English. Presents diversity of cultures coming together in America and displays contributions of each. Twenty 12½" x 17" posters in color depict Native, Black, Spanish-speaking, and Asian Americans; customs, foods, and celebrations. Order #68502.

National Association for the Education of Young Children.

Twelve 16" x 23" black and white posters of young children engaged in a variety of activities. Request publications brochure.

Records

Caedmon Records.

Request current catalog; see sections entitled "Black Studies" and "Folklore Around the World."

Children's Music Center.

Request catalogs: *Multi Ethnic Studies, North American Indians, History of Contribution of Black Americans*. Distributor of records by Hap Palmer, Ella Jenkins, and Pete Seeger, artists who are concerned with cultural awareness.

Children's Records of America.

Request catalog. Distributes "Sesame Street" records. Many deal with multicultural-bilingual situations.

Scholastic Book Services.

"Early Childhood" section of *Audio-Visual* catalog includes records and cassettes by Ella Jenkins. Also see "Games," "Rhythms and Songs," and "Language" sections.

Song of Many Cultures. Produced by Silver Burdett. Distributed by Time-Life.

Intercultural program resource. Some songs are suitable for kindergarten and primary children. Ten records with carrying case.

Songs for a Peaceful World. Produced and distributed by U.S. Committee for UNICEF.

Five songs on the theme of peace. Titles are "Let There Be Peace on Earth," "It Is Up to You and Me," "I'd Like to Teach the World to Sing," "Father of the Man," and "One Hundred Children."

Films/Filmstrips

Barr Films.

Request film catalog. Includes films related to personal and community problems and values, and explores responsibility. Grade level key provided.

A Beginning Collection: Guide to AV Materials. Baker & Taylor.

Filmstrips, posters, prints, annotated booklists, on Blacks, ethnic groups, folktales, music, and Africa for children in kindergarten through grade six.

Coronet Films.

Catalog lists multiethnic materials: filmstrips, records, cassettes. Children of diverse cultures are pictured using art to express feelings.

Department of Audiovisual Services, Brigham Young University.

Request 16 mm film rental catalog. See sections on Eskimos, African and Asian ethnic groups, Indians of North America and Mexico. Oriented toward adults and older children; however, some films can be used with young children. Young children delight in viewing the weaving, silversmithing, basketmaking, and potterymaking of the Hopis.

Folktales Around the World. Distributed by Baker & Taylor.

Stories from China, Japan, and Africa feature art and music. Sound filmstrips.

Free to Be? Produced and distributed by Anti-Defamation League of B'nai B'rith, 1977.

The purpose of this 16 mm film is to promote intergroup understanding. It raises questions about how free individuals are to be themselves amid the diversity and conformity of American life. For adults.

Greene, Ellen. **A Multimedia Approach to Children's Literature.** Distributed by American Library Association, 1972.

Excellent film resource.

It's O.K. for Me: It's O.K. for You. Produced and distributed by Paramount Communications.

Related filmstrip sets: *Learning about Me, Learning about Others, I Couldn't Care Less.* Four filmstrips/four cassettes with teacher's guide. Values, awareness, and responsibilities are explored through experiences of multiethnic groups.

Joanjo: A Portuguese Tale. Produced and distributed by Paramount Communications.

Life in a fishing village along the coast with a young child as the protagonist. Community working together to catch and prepare fish. Young boy dreams of having a life apart from "smelling fish" only to change his mind and return to the safety of his mother's lap. Soft monotone is difficult to follow; authentic setting interrupted by collage animation appeals to children. Twelve minutes, color, available for rental. Request list of rental libraries.

One Wonderful World. Produced and distributed by Paramount Communications.

Introduces young children to many lifestyles by showing homes, work, and recreation. Four filmstrips/four cassettes with teacher's guide.

Materials and Experiences

The Painting Ship. Produced and distributed by Weston Woods.

Documentary (13 minutes, color) presents an Amsterdam school, a floating workshop moored in the canal and designed to enable children to express creative artistic abilities as well as become more sensitive to their cultural environment. The film follows the children as they find expression through art, movement, music, and words.

Paramount Communications.

Sound filmstrips and catalog of "Materials for Bicultural/Bilingual Education." This distributor makes an effort to focus on integrated situations, nonracist materials. Superior in terms of considering minorities positively and fairly. Request catalog of materials for kindergarten through grade nine.

Pete and Penny's Pet Care. Produced and distributed by Paramount Communications.

Children learn responsibility for animals through experiences in and near Mr. Rodriquez's shop. Multiethnic groups. Four filmstrips/four cassettes with teacher's guide.

Phoenix Films.

Produce many exceptional films, some of which deal with minority concerns. Request their catalog of films.

Public and/or School Libraries.

See your local public and school libraries for audiovisual materials. Check under the name of each ethnic group in the subject card file. Librarians also solicit titles from citizens and teachers for purchase.

Pyramid Films.

Subject index for Black studies, geography, and American Indians; request rental catalog. Previews are available for prospective purchasers.

Society for Visual Education.

Catalog includes filmstrips for use with bilingual children. Black and Chicano images included. Discerning adult must evaluate how the content portrays a culture.

Texture Films.

Catalog lists some available films. Previews possible. *Anansi, the Spider* and *Arrow to the Sun*, both by Gerald McDermott, are available for rental.

William, Andy and Ramon and Five Friends at School. Holt, Rinehart and Winston, 1967.

A multiethnic series of stories about school and related children's activities. Children learn where each boy lives and where his parents work. Photography is excellent; audio ranges from good to fair. Six filmstrips in color, three cassettes, teacher's guide. For children ages four through seven.

With Pride to Progress: The Minority Child. Produced and distributed by Parents' Magazine Films, 1976.

This series of filmstrips for use with primary children and adults was designed to aid adults who are involved in the lives of young minority children. They can help these young children meet the challenges of contemporary life without abandoning their cultural traditions, beliefs, and concepts, so valuable to the development of a true sense of self-worth. The content emphasizes meeting developmental needs of and understanding the cultural influences on young minority children. Four color sets of filmstrips with records or cassettes. Each set contains five filmstrips with sound, five audio script booklets, and a discussion guide. The filmstrips are:

The Black Child, script by James P. Comer, Professor of Psychiatry at the Yale University Child Study Center.

The Chicano Child, script by Nathaniel Archuleta, Senior Project Director of the National Child Development Associate Program, College of Education, University of New Mexico.

The Indian Child, script by Winona Sample, a Redlake Chippewa, Curriculum Specialist for the Early Education Project at Haskell Indian Junior College.

The Puerto Rican Child, script by Aixa Figueroa de Berlin, Director of PRACA Bilingual-Bicultural Center in New York City; editorial assistant, Pedro F. Urbiztonda, doctoral student at New York University.

Slides

ROLOC Color Slides.

Mammouth collection on nature, animals, famous paintings, and events reflecting customs. Request price list.

Dolls

Children's Music Center.

"Music Center will make hand-sewn male and female dolls (with anatomically realistic bodies) to represent Black and other minority cultures."

Museums

Texas Museums Directory. Texas Historical Commission.

Includes 310 organized and permanent nonprofit institutions, essentially educational or aesthetic in purpose, which exhibit objects with intrinsic value to science, history, art, or culture, and which are open to the public. Check your state museums.

Resource Directory

This resource directory is provided for your convenience in requesting catalogs and further information about materials and resources listed in this book. Orders for materials may be placed directly with the publisher/distributor, your local bookstore, or your local school supply company. Addresses of publishers may change, and materials may go out of print.

Resource Directory

Aardvark Media, Inc.
975-B Detroit Ave.
Concord, CA 94518

ABC Records
Templeton Publishing Co., Inc.
New York, NY 10010

Abingdon Press
201 Eighth Ave., S.
Nashville, TN 37203

Harry N. Abrams
110 E. 59th St.
New York, NY 10022

Academic Press
111 Fifth Ave.
New York, NY 10003

ACI Films
Distribution Center
P.O. Box 1898
12 Jules Ln.
New Brunswick, NJ 08902

Addison-Wesley Publishing Co., Inc.
Reading, MA 01867

Advisory Committee on Education of Spanish and Mexican Americans
400 Maryland Ave., S.W.
Washington, DC 20202

Aeromexico (Aeronaves de Mexico)
8400 N.W. 52nd St.
Suite 100
Miami, FL 33166

African-American Institute
833 United Nations Plaza
New York, NY 10017

Afro-American Publishing Co., Inc.
1727 S. Indiana Ave.
Chicago, IL 60616

Alabama Bureau of Publicity and Information
State Capitol
Montgomery, AL 36104

Alaska Northwest Publishing Co.
Box 4EEE
Anchorage, AK 99505

Albuquerque Chamber of Commerce
Tourist Department
400 Elm St., N.E.
Albuquerque, NM 87102

Alternatives
1924 E. Third
Bloomington, IN 47401

American Federation of Arts
41 E. 65th St.
New York, NY 10021

American Film Co.
Paramount Oxford Films
5451 Marathon St.
Hollywood, CA 90038

American Folklore Society
University of Texas at El Paso
El Paso, TX 79968

American Heritage Publishing Co.
(Subsidiary of McGraw-Hill Book Co.)
1221 Avenue of the Americas
New York, NY 10020

American Indian Curriculum Development Program
3315 S. Airport Rd.
Bismarck, ND 58501

American Indian Historical Society
Indian Historian Press
1451 Masonic Ave.
San Francisco, CA 94117

American Library Association
50 E. Huron St.
Chicago, IL 60611

American Museum of Natural History
Central Park West at 79th St.
New York, NY 10024

American Speech and Hearing Association
9030 Old Georgetown Rd.
Washington, DC 20014

Amherst Asian American Committee
P.O. Box 370
Amherst, MA 01059

Anacostia Neighborhood Museum
2405 Martin Luther King, Jr., Ave., S.E.
Washington, DC 20020

Anti-Defamation League of B'nai B'rith
Book Department
315 Lexington Ave.
New York, NY 10016

Nathaniel Archuleta
University of New Mexico at Albuquerque
Albuquerque, NM 87131

Ariel Books
Serendipity Book Distribution
1790 Shattuck Ave.
Berkeley, CA 94709

Arizona Center for Educational Research and Development
College of Education
University of Arizona
Tucson, AZ 85721

Arizona State Museum
University of Arizona
Tucson, AZ 85721

Arizona State University
Hayden Library
Tempe, AZ 85281

Arno Press
330 Madison Ave.
New York, NY 10017

Asian American Bilingual Center
2168 Shattuck Ave.
Berkeley, CA 94704

Asian American Studies Center
3232 Campbell Hall
University of California, Los Angeles
Los Angeles, CA 90024

Asian American Studies Central, Inc.
1601 Griffith Park Blvd.
Los Angeles, CA 90026

Asian Multi-Media Center
1608 E. Jefferson St.
Seattle, WA 98122

Association for Asian Studies
Service Center for Teachers
Ohio State University
28 W. Woodruff Ave.
Columbus, OH 43210

Association for Childhood Education International
3615 Wisconsin Ave., N.W.
Washington, DC 20016

Association for the Study of Negro Life and History
1538 Ninth St., N.W.
Washington, DC 20001

Association of Children's Librarians
101 Lincoln Ave.
Daly City, CA 94015

Association of Chinese Teachers
641 Golden Gate Ave.
San Francisco, CA 94102

Association of Teacher Educators
1701 K St., N.W.
Washington, DC 20006

Atheneum Publishers
122 E. 42nd St.
New York, NY 10017

Atlanta University
School of Library Service
Atlanta, GA 30314

BABEL Resource Center
2168 Shattuck Ave.
2nd Floor
Berkeley, CA 94704

The Baker & Taylor Co.
Drawer Z
Momence, IL 60954

Ballantine Books, Inc.
(Division of Intext Publishing Group)
101 Fifth Ave.
New York, NY 10003

Bantam Books, Inc.
414 E. Golf Rd.
Des Plaines, IL 60016

Richard W. Baron
201 Park Ave., S.
New York, NY 10003

Barre Publishers
South St.
Barre, MA 01005

Barr Films
Box 5667
Pasadena, CA 91107

Basement Workshop, Inc.
22 Catherine St.
New York, NY 10038

Bay Area Bilingual Education League of the Berkeley California United School District Bilingual Project (BABEL)
Berkeley United School District
1414 Walnut St.
Berkeley, CA 94701

Beacon Press
25 Beacon St.
Boston, MA 02108

Bee Cross Media, Inc.
36 Dogwood Glen
Rochester, NY 14625

Behavorial Research Laboratories
Box 577
Palo Alto, CA 94302

Bibliographic Research and Collection Development Unit
Chicano Studies Center
University of California,
  Los Angeles
405 Hilgard Ave.
Los Angeles, CA 90024

Bilingual/Bicultural Resource Center
University of Southwestern
  Louisiana
P.O. Box 4-3410 USL
Lafayette, LA 70504

Bilingual Children's Television
2150 Valdez St.
Oakland, CA 94612

Bilingual Educational Services, Inc.
P.O. Box 669
1603 Hope St.
S. Pasadena, CA 91030

Bilingual Education Resource Center
College of Education
University of New Mexico
Albuquerque, NM 87131

Bilingual Education Service Center
500 S. Dwyer Ave.
Arlington Heights, IL 60005

Black History Exhibit Center
Nassau County Museum
106 N. Main St.
Hempstead, Long Island, NY 11550

Black Information Index
P.O. Box 332
Herndon, VA 22070

Bobbs-Merrill Co.
(Subsidiary of Howard W. Sams
  and Co., Inc.)
4300 W. 62nd St.
Indianapolis, IN 46268

Borrego Springs Chamber of Commerce
P.O. Box 66
Borrego Springs, CA 92004

Bowker Press
131 Washington Ave.
Portland, ME 04101

Bowmar
622 Rodier Dr.
Glendale, CA 91201

Bradbury Press, Inc.
2 Overhill Rd.
Scarsdale, NY 10583

Brooks/Cole Publishing Co.
(Division of Wadsworth Publishing
  Co.)
540 Abrego St.
Monterey, CA 93940

William C. Brown and Co.
135 S. Locust
Dubuque, IA 52001

Bureau of American Ethnology
Smithsonian Institution
Washington, DC 20560

Bureau of Indian Affairs
1951 Constitution Ave., N.W.
Washington, DC 20242

Aberdeen Area Office
115 4th Ave., S.E.
Aberdeen, SD 57401

Albuquerque Area Office
P.O. Box 8327
Albuquerque, NM 87103

Anadarko Area Office
Federal Bldg.
Anadarko, OK 73005

Billings Area Office
316 N. 26th St.
Billings, MT 59101

Eastern Area Office
1951 Constitution Ave., N.W.
Washington, DC 20242

Juneau Area Office
P.O. Box 3-8000
Juneau, AK 99802

Minneapolis Area Office
831 Second Ave., S.
Minneapolis, MN 55402

Muskogee Area Office
Federal Bldg.
Muskogee, OK 74401

Navajo Area Office
P.O. Box 1060
Gallup, NM 87301

Phoenix Area Office
P.O. Box 7007
Phoenix, AZ 85011

Resource Directory

Portland Area Office
P.O. Box 3785
Portland, OR 97208

Sacramento Area Office
Federal Office Bldg.
2800 Cottage Way
Sacramento, CA 95825

Caedmon Records, Inc.
2700 N. Richard Ave.
Indianapolis, IN 46219

Caldmon Records, Inc.
404 Eighth Ave.
New York, NY 10018

California Association of School Librarians
P.O. Box 1277
Burlingame, CA 94010

California State Department of Education
P.O. Box 271
Sacramento, CA 95803

California State University
Asian Studies Department
Long Beach, CA 90801

California State University
Chicano Research Library
5151 State College Dr.
Los Angeles, CA 90032

Caper Records
6100 Cherrylawn Cir.
Austin, TX 78723

Canyon Records
4143 N. 16th St.
Phoenix, AZ 85016

Cellar Book Shop
18090 Wyoming
Detroit, MI 48221

Center for Applied Linguistics
1611 N. Kent St.
Arlington, VA 22209

Center for Latin American Studies
Stanford University
Palo Alto, CA 94305

Center for Urban Education
University of Nebraska at Omaha
3805 N. 16th St.
Omaha, NE 68110

Center of Chicanos Studies Publications
Centro de Estudios Chicanos
San Diego State College
5402 College Ave.
San Diego, CA 92115

Centro de Estudios Puertorriqueños
City University of New York
500 Fifth Ave., Rm. 930
New York, NY 10036

Chappell and Co., Inc.
609 Fifth Ave.
New York, NY 10017

Chicago Convention and Tourism Bureau, Inc.
332 S. Michigan Ave.
Chicago, IL 60604

Chicago Natural History Museum
Department of Anthropology
Roosevelt Rd. & Lakeshore Dr.
Chicago, IL 60605

Chicano Cultural Center
University of California,
  Los Angeles
405 Hilgard Ave.
Los Angeles, CA 90024

Chicano Studies
University of New Mexico
Albuquerque, NM 87106

Chicano Studies Center
University of California,
  Los Angeles
405 Hilgard Ave.
Los Angeles, CA 90024

Chief Hawk at Setting Sun — United Remnant Band
Shawnee Nation
318 N. Tacoma St.
Indianapolis, IN 46201

Childcraft Education Corporation
20 Kilmer Rd.
Edison, NJ 08817

Children's Book & Music Center
5373 W. Pico Blvd.
Los Angeles, CA 90019

Children's Music Center, Inc.
5373 W. Pico Blvd.
Los Angeles, CA 90019

Children's Press
(Division of Regensteiner
  Publishing)
1224 W. Van Buren St.
Chicago, IL 60607

Children's Records of America, Inc.
159 W. 53rd St.
New York, NY 10019

Children's Television Workshop
North Rd.
Poughkeepsie, NY 12601

China Airlines, Ltd.
North American Headquarters
391 Sutter St.
San Francisco, CA 94108

China Books and Periodicals
125 Fifth Ave.
New York, NY 10003

China (Taiwan), Embassy of the Republic of
2311 Massachusetts Ave., N.W.
Washington, DC 20008

China Institute of America
125 E. 65th St.
New York, NY 10021

Chinese Bilingual Pilot Project
San Francisco United School
  District
135 Van Ness Ave.
San Francisco, CA 94102

Chinese for Affirmative Action
Chinese Media Committee
669 Clay St.
San Francisco, CA 94111

Chinese Information Service
159 Lexington Ave.
New York, NY 10016

Chujoda Publishing and Printing
Chiyoda-Shobo
Kanda-Junbo-Cho 1-23
Chujoda-ku
Tokyo, Japan

Andy Chuka Printers
Phoenix, AZ 85026

Citation Press
Scholastic Book Services
50 W. 44th St.
New York, NY 10036

College Entrance Examination Board
888 Seventh Ave.
New York, NY 10019

Resource Directory

Columbia Records
51 W. 52nd St.
New York, NY 10019

Constructive Playthings (U.S. Toys)
1040 E. 85th St.
Kansas City, MO 64131

David C. Cook Publishing Co.
School Products Division
850 N. Grove Ave.
Elgin, IL 60120

Coronet Films
65 E. South Water St.
Chicago, IL 60601

Coronet Media
65 E. South Water St.
Chicago, IL 60601

The Council on Interracial Books for Children, Inc.
1841 Broadway
New York, NY 10023

Coward, McCann & Geoghegan, Inc.
200 Madison Ave.
New York, NY 10016

C. P. Records
7291 Pacific View Dr.
Los Angeles, CA 90028

Creative Communications
1236 S. Main St.
Racine, WI 53403

Jack L. Crowder
Box 278
Bernalillo, NM 87004

Thomas Y. Crowell
666 Fifth Ave.
New York, NY 10019

Crowell Collier and Macmillan, Inc.
866 Third Ave.
New York, NY 10022

Crown Publishers, Inc.
419 Park Ave., S.
New York, NY 10016

Cruzada Spanish Publications
P.O. Box 1269
Homestead, FL 33030

Curriculum Center
San Juan School District Indian Education
Box 431
Blanding, UT 84511

Dallas Intertribal Center
336½ W. Jefferson St.
Dallas, TX 75246

Dallas Museum of Fine Arts
Fair Park
Dallas, TX 75226

Dallas Public Library
1954 Commerce
Dallas, TX 75201

Day Care and Child Development Council of America
1012 14th St., N.W.
Washington, DC 20005

John Day Co., Inc.
257 Park Ave., S.
New York, NY 10010

Delacorte Press
Dell Publishing Co., Inc.
750 Third Ave.
New York, NY 10017

Denver Museum of Natural History
City Park
Denver, CO 80206

Department of Foreign Languages
York College, CUNY
Jamaica, NY 11451

Developmental Learning Materials
7440 Natchez Ave.
Niles, IL 60648

Dial Press, Inc.
750 Third Ave.
New York, NY 10017

Dissemination and Assessment Center for Bilingual Bicultural Education
Educational Service Center
Region XIII
7703 N. Lamar
Austin, TX 78752

Dodd, Mead and Co.
79 Madison Ave.
New York, NY 10016

Doncel
Perez Ayuso 20
Madrid 2, Spain

Doubleday and Co., Inc.
245 Park Ave.
New York, NY 10017

Dover Publications
180 Varick St.
New York, NY 10014

E. P. Dutton and Co., Inc.
201 Park Ave., S.
New York, NY 10003

Early Years
Allen Raymond Inc.
P.O. Box 1223
Darien, CT 06820

Ebony Jr.!
Johnson Publishing Co.
1820 S. Michigan Ave.
Chicago, IL 60616

The Economics Press, Inc.
12 Daniel Rd.
Fairfield, NJ 07006

Educational Activities, Inc.
P.O. Box 392
Freeport, NY 11520

Educational Leadership
1701 K St., N.W.
Suite 1100
Washington, DC 20006

Educational Media Services
Brigham Young University
290 Herald R. Clark Bldg.
Provo, UT 84602

Educational Resources Information Center (ERIC) Clearinghouses

ERIC Clearinghouse on Career Education
Center for Vocational Education
Ohio State University
1960 Kenny Rd.
Columbus, OH 43210

ERIC Clearinghouse on Counseling and Personnel Services
The University of Michigan
School of Education Bldg., Rm. 2108
E. University & S. University
Ann Arbor, MI 48109

Resource Directory

ERIC Clearinghouse on Early
    Childhood Education (ERIC/
    ECE)
University of Illinois
805 W. Pennsylvania Ave.
Urbana, IL 61801

ERIC Clearinghouse on
    Educational Management
University of Oregon
Eugene, OR 97403

ERIC Clearinghouse on
    Handicapped and Gifted
    Children
Council for Exceptional Children
1920 Association Dr.
Reston, VA 22091

ERIC Clearinghouse on Higher
    Education
George Washington University
1 Dupont Cir., Suite 630
Washington, DC 20036

ERIC Clearinghouse on
    Information Resources
School of Education
Syracuse University
Syracuse, NY 13210

ERIC Clearinghouse on Junior
    Colleges
University of California
96 Powell Library Bldg.
Los Angeles, CA 90024

ERIC Clearinghouse on Languages
    and Linguistics
Center for Applied Linguistics
1611 N. Kent St.
Arlington, VA 22209

ERIC Clearinghouse on Reading
    and Communication Skills
1111 Kenyon Rd.
Urbana, IL 61801

ERIC Clearinghouse on Rural
    Education and Small Schools
New Mexico State University,
    Box 3AP
Las Cruces, NM 88003

ERIC Clearinghouse on Science,
    Mathematics, and Environmental
    Education
Ohio State University
1200 Chambers Rd., 3rd Floor
Columbus, OH 43212

ERIC Clearinghouse on Social
    Studies/Social Science
    Education
855 Broadway
Boulder, CO 80302

ERIC Clearinghouse on Teacher
    Education
1 Dupont Cir., Suite 616
Washington, DC 20036

ERIC Clearinghouse on Tests,
    Measurement, and Evaluation
Educational Testing Service
Princeton, NJ 08540

ERIC Clearinghouse on Urban
    Education
Teachers College, Box 40
Columbia University
New York, NY 10027

El Dorado Distributors
2489 Mission St., Suite 17
San Francisco, CA 94110

El Paso Schools
6531 Boling Dr.
El Paso, TX 79998

Encino Press
2003 S. Lamar
Austin, TX 78704

**Encyclopaedia Britannica
    Educational Corporation, Inc.**
425 N. Michigan Ave.
Chicago, IL 60611

Enterprises Publications
Newspaper Enterprise Association
230 Park Ave.
New York, NY 10017

EPIE Institute
375 Riverside Dr.
New York, NY 10027

**ERIC Document Reproduction
    Service**
P.O. Box 190
Arlington, VA 22210

Everybody's Bookstore
846 Kearny St.
San Francisco, CA 94108

**Far West Laboratory for Educational
    Research and Development**
1855 Folsom Rd.
San Francisco, CA 94103

Farrar, Straus and Giroux
19 Union Square W.
New York, NY 10003

Fawcett Publications
Fawcett World Library
1515 Broadway
New York, NY 10036

Fearon Publishers
(Industrial Division of Lear Siegler,
    Inc.)
6 Davis Dr.
Belmont, CA 94002

Fideler Co.
31 Ottawa Ave., N.W.
Grand Rapids, MI 49502

**Field Enterprises Educational
    Corporation**
510 Merchandise Mart Pl.
Chicago, IL 60654

**Filipino Youth Activities of
    Seattle, Inc.**
1608 E. Jefferson St.
Seattle, WA 98122

Filter Press
Box 5
Palmer Lake, CO 80133

Fisk University Library
Fisk University
Nashville, TN 37203

Folkways Scholastic Records
906 Sylvan Ave.
Englewood Cliffs, NJ 07632

Follett Publishing Co.
1010 W. Washington Blvd.
Chicago, IL 60607

Four Winds Press
(Division of Scholastic Magazines)
50 W. 44th St.
New York, NY 10036

Free Press
(Division of Macmillan Co.)
866 Third Ave.
New York, NY 10022

Funk and Wagnalls Co.
666 Fifth Ave.
New York, NY 10019

Fun Publishing Co.
P.O. Box 2049
Scottsdale, AZ 85252

Gale Research Co.
Book Tower
Detroit, MI 48226

Garrard Publishing Co.
1607 N. Market St.
Champaign, IL 61820

**General Learning Corporation/
    Silver Burdett**
250 James St.
Morristown, NJ 07960

Resource Directory

Golden Gate Junior Books
8344 Melrose Ave.
Los Angeles, CA 90069

Golden Press
Western Publishing Co., Inc.
1220 Mound Ave.
Racine, WI 53404

Greater Boston Chamber of Commerce
125 High
Boston, MA 02110

Great Plains Museum of Black History
2213 Lake St.
Omaha, NE 68110

Stephen Greene Press
Fessenden Rd.
Box 1000
Brattleboro, VT 05301

Greenwood Press
51 Riverside Ave.
Westport, CT 06880

Grosset and Dunlap, Inc.
51 Madison Ave.
New York, NY 10010

Grove Press, Inc.
196 W. Houston St.
New York, NY 10014

Gryphon House
P.O. Box 246
Mt. Rainier, MD 20822

G. K. Hall and Co.
70 Lincoln St.
Boston, MA 02111

Harcourt Brace Jovanovich, Inc.
757 Third Ave.
New York, NY 10017

Harper & Row Publishers
10 E. 53rd St.
New York, NY 10022

Haskell Institute
Publication Services
Lawrence, KS 66044

Hastings House Publishers, Inc.
10 E. 40th St.
New York, NY 10016

Heritage House
Box 7447
Albuquerque, NM 87104

Hill and Wang, Inc.
19 Union Square
New York, NY 10003

Hispanic-American Institute
100 E. 27th St.
Austin, TX 78705

Holiday House, Inc.
18 E. 56th St.
New York, NY 10022

Holt Rinehart and Winston, Inc.
(Subsidiary of Columbia Broadcasting System)
383 Madison Ave.
New York, NY 10017

Hopi Cultural Center Museum
P.O. Box 12
Second Mesa, AZ 86043

Hopi Publishers
Hopi Action Program
Oraibi, AZ 86039

Hopi Reservation
Follow Through
Oraibi, AZ 86039

Hopi Silvercraft Cooperative Guild
P.O. Box 37
Second Mesa, AZ 86043

The Hopi Tribe
P.O. Box 123
Oraibi, AZ 86039

Houghton Mifflin Co.
2 Park St.
Boston, MA 02107

Howard University Gallery of Art
2455 Sixth St., N.W.
Washington, DC 20001

Hubbard Press
2855 Sherimer Rd.
Northbrook, IL 60062

Hurting Publisher
10451 Jasper Ave.
Edmonton, Alberta
Canada

Iaconi Book Imports
300A Pennsylvania Ave.
San Francisco, CA 94109

ICBD
Publications Office
College of Education
University of Illinois
805 W. Pennsylvania Ave.
Urbana, IL 61801

Import Publishers
175 W. Moana Ln.
P.O. Box 6567
Reno, NV 89513

Indian America
P.O. Box 52009
Tulsa, OK 74152

Indian Arts and Crafts Board
Rm. 4004
U.S. Department of the Interior
Washington, DC 20240

Indiana University Northwest
3400 Broadway
Gary, IN 46408

Indiana University Press
10th & Morton Sts.
Bloomington, IN 47401

Indiana University of South Bend
1825 Northside Blvd.
South Bend, IN 46615

Indian Cultural/Curriculum Center
Tuba City Public Schools
Tuba City, AZ 86045

Indian Education Resources Center
123 Fourth St., S.W.
P.O. Box 1788
Albuquerque, NM 87103

Indian Historian Press
1451 Masonic Ave.
San Francisco, CA 94117

Indian House
Box 472
Taos, NM 87571

Inland Library System
Riverside City and County Public Library
San Bernardino and Riverside Counties
3581 Seventh St.
P.O. Box 468
Riverside, CA 92502

Institute for Minnesota Indians
WISC Library Services
University of Minnesota
2400 Oakland Ave.
Duluth, MN 55812

Institute of Latin American Studies
University of Texas Campus
Austin, TX 78712

Institute of Modern Languages
2622 Pittman Dr.
Silver Spring, MD 20910

Resource Directory

Institute of Texas Cultures
P.O. Box 1226
San Antonio, TX 78294

Instructional Challenges Inc.
P.O. Box 665
Fairview, NM 87532

Instructional Service Center
Professional Library
P.O. Box 66
Brigham City, UT 84302

Integrated Education Associates
343 S. Dearborn St.
Chicago, IL 60604

Inter-American Indian Institute
General Secretariat
Pan American Union
17th and Constitution Ave., N.W.
Washington, DC 20036

International Learning Systems, Inc.
1715 Connecticut Ave., N.W.
Washington, DC 20009

Island Heritage Limited Editorial Offices
1020 Auaki St., Bldg. 3
Honolulu, HI 96814

Japan Air Lines
North American Headquarters
655 Fifth Ave.
New York, NY 10022

Japan, Embassy of
2520 Massachusetts Ave., N.W.
Washington, DC 20008

Japanese American Citizens' League
526 S. Jackson St.
Seattle, WA 98104

Japanese American Curriculum Project
P.O. Box 367
San Mateo, CA 94401
Store:
414 E. Third Ave.
San Mateo, CA 94401

Japan House Gallery
333 E. 47th St.
New York, NY 10017

Japan National Tourist Organization
45 Rockefeller Plaza
New York, NY 10020
and
1420 Commerce St.
Dallas, TX 75201

Japan Publishing Trading Co., Ltd.
Central P.O. Box 722
Tokyo, Japan

Johnson Publishing Co.
1820 S. Michigan Ave.
Chicago, IL 60616

Judson Press
Valley Forge, PA 19481

Julesberg Historical Museum
320 Cedar
Julesberg, CO 80737

K. C. Publications
Box 14883
Las Vegas, NV 89114

Kendall/Hunt Publishing Co.
Dubuque, IA 52001

Keyboard Publications, Inc.
1346 Chapel St.
New Haven, CT 06511

Pete Kitchen Western Museum
U. S. Highway 90
Nogales, AZ 85621

Neil A. Kjos Music Co.
525 Busse
Park Ridge, IL 60068

Alfred A. Knopf, Inc.
(Subsidiary of Random House, Inc.)
201 E. 50th St.
New York, NY 10022

Koshare Indian Kiva Art Museum
18th and Santa Fe Aves.
La Junta, CO 81050

La Luz
8000 E. Girard
Suite 314
Denver, CO 80231

Lane Magazine and Book Co.
Menlo Park, CA 94025

Larousse and Co., Inc.
572 Fifth Ave.
New York, NY 10036

Las Américas Publishing Co.
37 Union Sq. W.
New York, NY 10003

Libraries Unlimited, Inc.
Colorado Bibliographic Institute
Box 263
Littleton, CO 80120

Library Promotionals
Box 976
Hagerstown, MD 21740

Libreria Alma Mater
Cabrera Numero 867
Rio Piedras, Puerto Rico 00928

LINC Child Development Training Center
800 Silver Ave.
Greensboro, NC 27403

LINC Leadership Development Program
1001 N. Elm St.
Greensboro, NC 27401

Lion Press
21 W. 38th St.
New York, NY 10018

J. B. Lippincott Co.
E. Washington Sq.
Philadelphia, PA 19105

Little, Brown and Co., Inc.
34 Beacon St.
Boston, MA 02106

Longmans, Green and Co., Inc.
55 Fifth Ave.
New York, NY 10003

Los Angeles County Museum of Natural History
900 Exposition Blvd.
Los Angeles, CA 90007

Lothrop, Lee and Shepard Co.
105 Madison Ave.
New York, NY 10016

Robert H. Lowie Museum of Anthropology
University of California
Kroeber Hall
Bancroft Way and College Ave.
Berkeley, CA 94720

Lyons
530 Riverview Ave.
Elkhart, IN 46514

Resource Directory

McGraw-Hill Book Co.
1221 Avenue of the Americas
New York, NY 10020

McNally and Loftin Publishers
111 E. De La Guerra St.
Box 1316
Santa Barbara, CA 93102

Macmillan Co.
866 Third Ave.
New York, NY 10022

Macmillan Library Services
222 Brown St.
Riverside, NJ 08075

Edwards B. Marks Music Corporation
136 W. 52nd St.
New York, NY 10019

Mary Lois School of Dance
7126 Library Ln.
Dallas, TX 75232

Melmont Publishers
(Subsidiary of Children's Press)
1224 W. Van Buren St.
Chicago, IL 60607

Mentor Books
New American Library
1301 Avenue of the Americas
New York, NY 10019

Julian Messner
(Division of Simon and Schuster)
1 W. 39th St.
New York, NY 10018

Mexicana Airlines
United States Headquarters
851 Burlway Rd., Suite 600
Burlingame, CA 94010

Mexican Chamber of Commerce of the United States
60 Wall St.
New York, NY 10005

Mexican Embassy
2829 16th St., N.W.
Washington, DC 20009

Mexican Government Tourism Department
630 Fifth Ave., Suite 351
New York, NY 10020
and
1800 Main St.
Shop B
Dallas, TX 75201
and
3106 Wilshire Blvd.
Los Angeles, CA 90010

Mexican National Tourist Council
677 Fifth Ave.
New York, NY 10022
and
1 Shell Plaza
Houston, TX 77002

Michigan Education Association
Publications
P.O. Box 673
E. Lansing, MI 48823

Miller-Brody Productions, Inc.
342 Madison Ave.
New York, NY 10017

Mills and Boon Ltd.
17-19 Foley St.
London, England

Modern Language Association of America
62 Fifth Ave.
New York, NY 10011

Modern Talking Picture Service
2323 New Park Rd.
Hyde Park, NY 11040

Mohawk Nation
via Rooseveltown, NY 13683

Moreno Education Co.
7050 Belle Glade Ln.
San Diego, CA 92119

William Morrow and Co.
105 Madison Ave.
New York, NY 10016

Multicultural Resources
P.O. Box 2945
Stanford, CA 94305

Multilingual Multicultural Resource and Training Center of New England
Summit Avenue School
8-6 Fourth St.
Providence, RI 02906

Museum of African Art
316-318 A St., N.E.
Washington, DC 20002

Museum of the American Indian Heye Foundation
Broadway & 155th
New York, NY 10032

Museum of New Mexico
Palace Ave.
Santa Fe, NM 87501

Museum of New Mexico Press
Box 2087
Santa Fe, NM 87501

Museum of Northern Arizona
Box 1389
Flagstaff, AZ 86001

National Art Education Association
1201 16th St., N.W.
Washington, DC 20036

National Assessment and Dissemination Center for Bilingual/Bicultural Education
385 High St.
Fall River, MA 02720

National Association for the Education of Young Children
1834 Connecticut Ave., N.W.
Washington, DC 20009

National Collection of Fine Arts
8th and G Sts., N.W.
Washington, DC 20001

National Conference of Christians and Jews
43 W. 57th St.
New York, NY 10019

National Council of Teachers of English
1111 Kenyon Rd.
Urbana, IL 61801

National Educational Laboratory Publishers, Inc.
P.O. Box 1003
Austin, TX 78767

National Geographic Society
17th and M Sts., N.W.
Washington, DC 20036

National Indian Education Association
Hubbard Bldg., Suite 200
2675 University Ave.
St. Paul, MN 55114

National Museum of Natural History
Smithsonian Institution
10th and Constitution Ave., N.W.
Washington, DC 20001

Resource Directory

National Textbook Co.
8259 Niles Center Rd.
Skokie, IL 60076

Native American Solidarity Committee
P.O. Box 3426
St. Paul, MN 55165

Naturegraph Publishers
8339 W. Dry Creek Rd.
Healdsburg, CA 95448

Navajo Arts and Crafts Guild
Box 8
Window Rock, AZ 86515

Navajo Curriculum Center
Star Route #1
P.O. Box 246
Many Farms, AZ 86538

Navajo Curriculum Center Press
Box 804
Blanding, UT 84551

Navajo Nation
College Bookstore
Navajo Community College
Tsaile Campus
Chinle, AZ 86556

Navajo Reading Study
The University of New Mexico
Albuquerque, NM 87131

Navajo Tribal Museum
P.O. Box 769
Window Rock, AZ 86515

The Navajo Tribe
Window Rock, AZ 86515

The Naylor Co.
1015 Culebra Ave.
San Antonio, TX 78296

Thomas Nelson & Sons, Inc.
Copewood and Davis Sts.
Camden, NJ 08103

New Mexico Magazine
113 Washington Ave.
Santa Fe, NM 87503

New Mexico State University Press
Las Cruces, NM 88003

New York Convention and Visitors Bureau
90 E. 42nd St.
New York, NY 10017

New York Graphic Society, Ltd.
140 Greenwich Ave.
Greenwich, CT 06830

The New York Public Library
The Branch Libraries
8 E. 40th St.
New York, NY 10016

New York Times Book Co.
330 Madison Ave.
New York, NY 10017

New York University Press
Washington Square
New York, NY 10003

Noble and Noble Publishers, Inc.
1 Dag Hammarskjold Plaza
245 E. 47th St.
New York, NY 10017

Northland Press
Box N
Flagstaff, AZ 86001

W. W. Norton and Co., Inc.
55 Fifth Ave.
New York, NY 10003

Oakland Museum
1000 Oak St.
Oakland, CA 94607

Oakland Unified School District
1025 Second Ave.
Oakland, CA 94606

Oceana Publications
Dobbs Ferry, NY 10522

ODDO Publishing Inc.
Fayetteville, GA 30214

Office of State Superintendent of Public Instruction
Old Capitol Bldg.
Olympia, WA 98504

J. Phillip O'Hara, Inc.
20 E. Huron St.
Chicago, IL 60611

Old Mission San Luis Rey
4050 Mission Ave.
San Luis Rey, CA 92068

Organization of American States
General Secretariat
Cultural Relations
Sales and Promotion Division
Washington, DC 20006

Other Options
4205 University Ave.
San Diego, CA 92105

Palms Trading Co.
1504 Lomas Blvd., N.W.
Albuquerque, NM 87104

Pantheon Books
(Division of Random House)
201 E. 50th St.
New York, NY 10022

Paramount Communications
5451 Marathon St.
Hollywood, CA 90038

Paredon Records
Box 889
Brooklyn, NY 11202

Parents' Magazine Films, Inc.
52 Vanderbilt Ave.
New York, NY 10017

Parents' Magazine Press
52 Vanderbilt Ave.
New York, NY 10017

Parnassus Press
2721 Parker St.
Berkeley, CA 94704

F. E. Peacock Publishers, Inc.
401 W. Irving Park Rd.
Itasca, IL 60143

Penca Books
1420 W. Commerce
P.O. Box 7407
San Antonio, TX 78207

People Against Racism in Education
Box 972
Cathedral Station
New York, NY 10025

Petley Studios
4051 E. Van Buren
Phoenix, AZ 85008

Philadelphia Convention and Visitors Bureau
1525 J.F. Kennedy Blvd.
Philadelphia, PA 19124

Phoenix Films, Inc.
470 Park Ave., S.
New York, NY 10016

Resource Directory

Jesús Gonzales Pita
1540 S.W. 14th Ter.
Miami, FL 33145

Platt and Munk Inc.
c/o Grosset & Dunlap
51 Madison Ave.
New York, NY 10010

Portland Public Schools
Educational Media Department
Portland, OR 97205

The Potomac Institute, Inc.
1501 18th St., N.W.
Washington, DC 20036

Prentice-Hall, Inc.
Englewood Cliffs, NJ 07632

Promontory Press
A and W Promotional Book
  Corporation
95 Madison Ave.
New York, NY 10016

The Proof Press
P.O. Box 1256
Berkeley, CA 94720

Proyecto Leer Bulletin
1736 Columbia Rd., N.W.
Suite 107
Washington, DC 20009

Public Art Workshop
5623 W. Madison St.
Chicago, IL 60644

Public Documents
Distribution Center
Pueblo, CO 81009

G. P. Putnam's Sons
200 Madison Ave.
New York, NY 10016

Pyramid Films
Box 1048
Santa Monica, CA 90406

**Quadrangle/The New York Times
  Book Co.**
330 Madison Ave.
New York, NY 10017

**Racism and Sexism Resource
  Center for Educators**
Council on Interracial Books for
  Children, Inc.
1841 Broadway
New York, NY 10023

Rand-McNally and Co.
Box 7600
Chicago, IL 60680

Random House
201 E. 50th St.
New York, NY 10022

**Regional Cross-Cultural Training
  and Resource Center**
New York City Board of Education
110 Livingston St.
Rm. 222
Brooklyn, NY 11201

Republic of China Tourism Bureau
210 Post St., Rm. 705
San Francisco, CA 94108

Ridge Press, Inc.
17 E. 45th St.
New York, NY 10017

Ward Ritchie Press
474 S. Arroyo Pkwy.
Pasadena, CA 91105

ROLOC Color Slides
P.O. Box 1715
Washington, DC 20013

Ronald Press Co.
79 Madison Ave.
New York, NY 10016

Rough Rock School Board, Inc.
Communication Office
Chinle, AZ 86503

Royal Thai Embassy
2300 Kalorama Rd., N.W.
Washington, DC 20008

Ruiz Productions, Inc.
3518 Cahaenga Blvd. W.
Suite 210
Hollywood, CA 90068

St. Augustine Chamber of Commerce
10 Castillo Dr.
St. Augustine, FL 32084

St. Martin's Press, Inc.
175 Fifth Ave.
New York, NY 10010

**San Diego Convention and Visitors
  Bureau**
1200 Third Ave., Suite 824
San Diego, CA 92101

San Diego State University
School of Education
5544½ Hardy Ave.
San Diego, CA 92182

**San Francisco Chamber of
  Commerce**
465 California
San Francisco, CA 92101

**San Francisco Convention and
  Visitors Bureau**
Fox Plaza
San Francisco, CA 94102

San Francisco State College
1600 Holloway
San Francisco, CA 94132

**San Jacinto Museum of History
  Association**
San Jacinto Battleground Park
P.O. Box 758
Deer Park, TX 77536

**San Juan Bautista State Historic
  Park**
Second St.
P.O. Box 116
San Juan Bautista, CA 95045

Scarecrow Press, Inc.
52 Liberty St.
Box 656
Metuchen, NJ 08840

Scholastic Audio Visual Center
904 Sylvan Ave.
Englewood Cliffs, NJ 07632

Scholastic Book Services
50 W. 44th St.
New York, NY 10036

Scholastic Records
906 Sylvan Ave.
Englewood Cliffs, NJ 07632

School of Library Service
Atlanta University
Atlanta, GA 30314

School Products Division
850 N. Grove Ave.
Elgin, IL 60120

Scottsbluff Chamber of Commerce
Scottsbluff, NE 69361

Charles Scribner's Sons
597 Fifth Ave.
New York, NY 10017

Resource Directory

Seabury Press, Inc.
815 Second Ave.
New York, NY 10017

Service Center for Teachers of Asian Studies
Ohio State University
29 W. Woodruff Ave.
Columbus, OH 43210

Shindana Toys
4161 S. Central
Los Angeles, CA 90011

Silver Burdett Co.
250 James St.
Morristown, NJ 07960

Simon and Schuster, Inc.
630 Fifth Ave.
New York, NY 10020

L. W. Singer Co.
1345 Diversey Pkwy.
Chicago, IL 60614

Sino-American Cultural Society
2000 P St., N.W.
Suite 200
Washington, DC 20036

Slater Memorial Museum
Norwich Free Academy
108 Crescent St.
Norwich, CT 06360

Slides Unlimited
1909 Bryan St.
P.O. Box 113
Dallas, TX 75221

Society for Visual Education, Inc.
1345 Diversey Pkwy.
Chicago, IL 60614

Southeast Museum of the North American Indian
P.O. Box 248
U.S. Hwy. 1
Marathon, FL 33050

Southern California Visitors Council
750 W. 7th St.
Los Angeles, CA 90017

Southern Methodist University/ National Conference of Christians and Jews
1027 Dallas Athletic Club Bldg.
Dallas, TX 75201

Southern Plains Indian Museum and Craft Center
Box 447
Anadarko, OK 73005

Southwest Educational Development Laboratory
211 E. 7th St.
Austin, TX 78701

Southwest Network
1020 B St., Suite 8
Hayward, CA 94541

Southwest Resource and Information Center
Box 4524
Albuquerque, NM 87106

Spanish Book Corporation of America
115 Fifth Ave.
New York, NY 10020

Spoken Arts
310 North Ave.
New Rochelle, NY 10801

Stallman Educational Systems, Inc.
P.O. Box AL
Roslyn Heights, NY 11577

Stanford Area Chinese Club
Service-Cultural Committee
P.O. Box 1147
Palo Alto, CA 94301

Steck-Vaughn Co.
Box 2028
Austin, TX 78767

Sterling Publishing Co., Inc.
419 Park Ave., S.
New York, NY 10016

R. H. Stone
13735 Puritan
Detroit, MI 48227

Sullivan's Associates
1801 Page Mill Rd.
Suite 210
Palo Alto, CA 94304

Sunstone Press
Box 2321
Santa Fe, NM 87501

Swallow Press, Inc.
1139 Wabash Ave.
Chicago, IL 60605

Tandem Press, Inc.
Box 237
Tannersville, PA 18372

Texas Department of Community Affairs
Early Childhood Development Division
P.O. Box 13166
Capitol Station
Austin, TX 78711

Texas Education Agency
201 E. 11th St.
Austin, TX 78701

Texas Folklore Society
University Station
Nacogdoches, TX 75961

Texas Historical Commission
Box 12276
Capitol Station
Austin, TX 78711

Texian Press
1301 Jefferson St.
Waco, TX 76702

Texture Films
1600 Broadway
New York, NY 10019

Thunderbird Records
Santa Fe, NM 87501

Time-Life Books
Rockefeller Center
New York, NY 10020

Todd Publications
11 Third St.
Rye, NY 10580

Tricontinental Film Center
333 Avenue of the Americas
New York, NY 10014
and
P.O. Box 4430
Berkeley, CA 94704

Tucson Festival Society
8 W. Paseo Redondo
Tucson, AZ 85705

Tumacacori National Monument
U. S. Hwy. 89
P.O. Box 67
Tumacacori, AZ 85621

Charles E. Tuttle Co.
28 S. Main St.
Rutland, VT 05701

Twayne Publishers
31 Union Square W.
New York, NY 10003

U. S. Commission on Civil Rights
Washington, DC 20425

U.S. Committee for UNICEF
331 E. 38th St.
New York, NY 10016

U.S. Department of Health, Education, and Welfare
Washington, DC 20201

U.S. Department of the Interior
Bureau of Indian Affairs
Indian Education Resources Center
123 Fourth St., S.W.
Albuquerque, NM 87103

U.S. Department of the Interior Museum
19th and C Sts., N.W.
Washington, DC 20240

U.S. Government Printing Office
Superintendent of Documents
Washington, DC 20402

Universal Education and Visual Arts
221 Park Ave., S.
New York, NY 10003

University of Arizona Press
Box 3398
Tucson, AZ 85722

UCLA Asian American Studies Center
3232 Campbell Hall
Los Angeles, CA 90024

University of Chicago Press
5801 Ellis Ave.
Chicago, IL 60637

University of Houston
3801 Cullen Blvd.
Houston, TX 77001

University of Illinois
College of Education
805 W. Pennsylvania Ave.
Urbana, IL 61801

University of Michigan Press
615 E. University
Ann Arbor, MI 48106

University of Nebraska Press
901 N. 17th St.
Lincoln, NE 68508

University of New Mexico Press
Albuquerque, NM 87106

University of Notre Dame Press
Notre Dame, IN 46556

University of Oklahoma Press
1005 Asp Ave.
Norman, OK 73069

University of Texas Press
Box 7819 University Station
Austin, TX 78712

University Press
Drawer N
Wolfe City, TX 75496

Urban Information Interpreters, Inc.
P.O. Box AH
College Park, MD 20740

Urban Media Materials
212 Mineola Ave.
Roslyn Heights, NY 11577

Vanguard Press, Inc.
424 Madison Ave.
New York, NY 10017

Van Nostrand Reinhold Co.
450 W. 33rd St.
New York, NY 10001

Viking Press, Inc.
625 Madison Ave.
New York, NY 10022

Villagra Book Shop
P.O. Box 460
Santa Fe, NM 87501

Vintage Books
201 E. 50th St.
New York, NY 10022

H. Z. Walck, Inc.
19 Union Square W.
New York, NY 10017

Walker and Co.
720 Fifth Ave.
New York, NY 10019

Frederick Warne and Co., Inc.
101 Fifth Ave.
New York, NY 10003

Washington Area Convention and Visitors Association
1129 20th St., N.W.
Washington, DC 20036

Washington Square Press
630 Fifth Ave.
New York, NY 10020

Franklin Watts, Inc.
(Subsidiary of Grolier)
845 Third Ave.
New York, NY 10022

John Weatherhill, Inc.
149 Madison Ave.
New York, NY 10016

Westernlore Press
5117 Eagle Rock Blvd.
Los Angeles, CA 90041

Western Publications, Inc.
P.O. Box 3338
Austin, TX 78764

Western Publishing Co., Inc.
1220 Mound Ave.
Racine, WI 53404

Weston Woods
Weston, CT 06883

Albert Whitman and Co.
560 W. Lake St.
Chicago, IL 60606

Wisconsin Department of Public Instruction
126 Langdon St.
Madison, WI 53702

Wonder Books
1107 Broadway
New York, NY 10010

Woodard's Indian Arts
224 W. Coal Ave.
Gallup, NM 87301

World Publishing Co.
110 E. 59th St.
New York, NY 10022

Peter H. Wyden
750 Third Ave.
New York, NY 10017

Xerox Book Catalogs Department
300 N. Zeeb Rd.
Ann Arbor, MI 48106

Yale University Press
92A Yale Station
New Haven, CT 06520

Brigham Young University
290 HRCB
Provo, UT 84602

Selected NAEYC Publications

If you found this book helpful, you may wish to order these and other NAEYC publications:

Code #	Title	Price
214	**Activities for School-Age Child Care,** by Rosalie Blau, Elizabeth H. Brady, Ida Bucher, Betsy Hiteshew, Ann Zavitkovsky, and Docia Zavitkovsky	$3.85
315	**Administration: Making Programs Work for Children and Families,** edited by Dorothy W. Hewes	$5.50
132	**The Block Book,** edited by Elisabeth S. Hirsch	$3.85
200	**Careers with Young Children: Making Your Decision,** by Judith W. Seaver, Carol A. Cartwright, Cecelia B. Ward, and C. Annette Heasley	$4.40
213	**Caring: Supporting Children's Growth,** by Rita M. Warren	$2.20
402S	**Cómo Reconocer un Buen Programa de Educación Pre-Escolar**	$ .30
119	**Curriculum Is What Happens: Planning Is the Key,** edited by Laura L. Dittmann	$2.20
121	**Developmental Screening in Early Childhood: A Guide,** by Samuel J. Meisels	$2.75
314	**Directory of Educational Programs for Adults Who Work with Children,** compiled by Dianne Rothenberg	$3.30
300	**Early Childhood Education: An Introduction to the Profession,** by James L. Hymes, Jr.	$1.65
108	**Education for Parenting,** by Mary B. Lane	$3.30
112	**Ethical Behavior in Early Childhood Education,** by Lillian G. Katz and Evangeline H. Ward	$2.00
215	**A Festival of Films**	$2.00
212	**A Good Beginning for Babies: Guidelines for Group Care,** by Anne Willis and Henry Ricciuti	$4.95
302	**A Guide to Discipline,** by Jeannette Galambos Stone	$1.65
210	**The Idea Box,** by Austin AEYC	$6.25
105	**Ideas That Work with Young Children, Vol. 2,** edited by Leah Adams and Betty Garlick	$4.70
101	**Let's Play Outdoors,** by Katherine Read Baker	$1.10
316	**More Than Graham Crackers: Nutrition Education and Food Preparation with Young Children,** by Nancy Wanamaker, Kristin Hearn, and Sherrill Richarz	$4.20
312	**Mother/Child, Father/Child Relationships,** edited by Joseph H. Stevens, Jr., and Marilyn Mathews	$5.20

Code #	Title	Price
308	**Mud, Sand, and Water,** by Dorothy M. Hill	$2.20
107	**Music in Our Lives: The Early Years,** by Dorothy T. McDonald	$2.75
135	**Parent Involvement in Early Childhood Education,** by Alice S. Honig	$3.30
102	**Piaget, Children, and Number,** by Constance Kamii and Rheta DeVries	$2.20
115	**Planning Environments for Young Children: Physical Space,** by Sybil Kritchevsky and Elizabeth Prescott, with Lee Walling	$2.00
306	**Play as a Learning Medium,** edited by Doris Sponseller	$3.00
129	**Play: The Child Strives Toward Self-Realization,** edited by Georgianna Engstrom	$2.75
126	**Promoting Cognitive Growth: A Developmental-Interaction Point of View,** by Barbara Biber, Edna Shapiro, and David Wickens, with Elizabeth Gilkeson	$3.00
309	**Science with Young Children,** by Bess-Gene Holt	$3.55
309A	**Doing a Workshop with an NAEYC Publication,** by Bess-Gene Holt	$1.00
128	**The Significance of the Young Child's Motor Development,** edited by Georgianna Engstrom	$2.45
402E	**Some Ways of Distinguishing a Good Early Childhood Program**	$ .30
310	**Talks with Teachers: Reflections on Early Childhood Education,** by Lilian G. Katz	$3.30
311	**Teaching Practices: Reexamining Assumptions,** edited by Bernard Spodek	$2.50

All prices include postage and handling. Please enclose full payment for orders under $10. Order from NAEYC
                         1834 Connecticut Ave., N.W.
                         Washington, DC 20009

For information about other NAEYC publications, write for a *free* publications brochure.

The journal *Young Children* is available through NAEYC membership or by subscription. Write to NAEYC for information.